Don't
stand up in the
Tunnel !

ISBN 1-900622-04-1 (Hardback)

British Library Cataloguing in Publication Data
Boyd J.I.C. (James Ian Craig), 1920 -
Don't Stand up in the Tunnel : The story of the Downs Light Railway & its young
Engineers
1. Downs School - History
2. Railroads, Miniature - England - Malvern - History
I. Title
625.1'9'0942447

Publishing, Typesetting, Design and Graphics by:
RailRomances Publishing, PO Box 85,
Chester. CH4 9ZH

Image Setting and Scanning by:
Lazertype, Laurel Bank,
Gresford, Wrexham LL12 8NT

Printed by:
The Amadeus Press Ltd.,
Ezra House, West 26 Business Park,
Cleckheaton. BD19 4TQ

Sponsored by:
This book has been jointly sponsored by Tim Cadbury,
Jim Hoyland and John Milner (RailRomances Publishing).

Don't stand up in the Tunnel !

The Story of The Downs Light Railway
and its young Engineers

1925 — 2001

'Aedificandum Est'

by

James I.C. Boyd

('Sir')

Rail Romances

PO Box 85, Chester. CH4 9ZH
UK

Foreword

James Boyd's long awaited history of The Downs Light Railway has truly been a labour of love, as has been all the work that he has done for the Railway over the past 30 years. The book tells the story of a unique partnership between a school and a miniature railway. James clearly fell in love with the Railway soon after he arrived at The Downs School as a 10 year old. He was one of ten licensed engine drivers in 1933 and at the same time he was being taught to be a writer by the then English master, W.H. Auden.

James' retirement to Colwall in 1970 was greeted with a huge sigh of relief. With the best will in the world the Railway had fallen into a sad state of disrepair. Not only has he got unrivalled knowledge of railways, he also has a genius for picking up spare parts from unlikely places and cajoling his friends into doing jobs for him.

In these days of tight budgetary control it is very difficult for a school to afford to maintain a railway. Thus in 1981 The Downs Light Railway Trust was formed to give the Railway some independence from the School. An appeal was sent out to all the Old Boys of the School, and their generous response was proof of their affection for the Railway. A number of railway experts have served as Trustees over the years under the Chairmanship firstly of John Hall-Craggs, then Tim Cadbury and finally Patrick Keef. Patrick is often to be seen down at the Railway helping James' young engineers. The School has good reason to be grateful for all that the Trust has done.

The Downs has thrown up many characters in its 100 year history, but none more colourful than James Boyd. He is clearly held in deep affection by his young engineers, and it is equally clear that he feels the same about them. Anyone supervising children at work on a railway must be a disciplinarian, but the children know that there is always a twinkle in 'Sir's' eye, however fierce he may sometimes appear to be. They have learnt to take him with just a tiny pinch of salt, as indeed have we all. He knows how to pull a leg or two! James is also an expert photographer, as was my father, Geoffrey Hoyland, the founder of the Railway, and the many photographs in this book will be greatly enjoyed, especially by Old Downians. They have been beautifully reproduced by John Milner, the publisher of the book. He is another Trustee who has contributed very generously to The Downs Light Railway.

It will be a sad day indeed when James finally learns the meaning of the word 'retirement'. Sad, not only for the School but also for the many people in the wider community who enjoy a day out on the Railway in his company. This involvement of the general public has been one of the Railway's strengths. Meanwhile, long may James enjoy his memories of the three important anniversaries of the year 2000; the centenary of the School, the 75th birthday of the Railway and, not least, the 30 years of his involvement with it.

H.J. Hoyland.

July 2001

Contents

An Appreciation

Over a period of seventy-five years, there are countless people who have assisted The Downs Light Railway and the Railway Trustees. In particular, the following should be mentioned : Donald C. Boyd, Derek Brimmell, E.J. Brown, Tim Cadbury, Geoffrey Davidson, Andrew Harris, H. James Hoyland, Patrick Keef, A.D. Lamberton, Norman Livingstone, John Milner, Hugh Nicklin, Francis Parker, Brian Rogers, Edwin Shearing, Tom Stephens, J.V. Terry, Don Taylour, John C. Wilkins, J.S. Wilkinson and Derek Williams.

Acknowledgements

Donald C. Boyd, Maurice H. Clark, C.R.S. Haslam, H. James Hoyland, David J. Payne, John Remington, Richard Webster and Alan Woodall who are all Old Downians, plus Bob Burgess, David Curwen, John Hall-Craggs, John Milner, Ronald (Bob) Morse, Simon Townsend and Rodney Weaver.

Dedication

To our grand-daughter
ANGELA ELIZABETH CRAIG O'SULLIVAN
for whom The Downs Light Railway has been a lifetime companion

Preface

The setting in time of this account begins in the age when every boy longed to be a steam locomotive driver when he grew up (or before, if opportunity offered). It was the time of the MECCANO MAGAZINE, THE MODEL ENGINEER, MODELS, RAILWAYS & LOCOMOTIVES and similar periodicals; all concerned creativity.

Model Engineering firms such as BASSETT-LOWKE or STUART TURNER who produced lavish handbooks and catalogues over which small boys might drool, catered for this market and lucky was the child whose parent could afford to buy the tempting objects which they proffered therein. The Author … frequently referred to as 'Sir' in these pages … was amongst those who drooled.

Herein one may read of a group of fortunate boys whose latent enthusiasm burgeoned under an enlightened Headmaster and who, in later life, have much for which to thank providence that they were among the privileged few. Happily, the story does not end with the termination of the Hoyland regime; boys and girls of edified parents still continue to benefit from the enlarged spectrum of education which the School offers.

The Author and Publisher respectfully advise readers that The Downs Light Railway is located within the private grounds of The Downs School and that there is no access to persons other than School Staff, Pupils and Parents. The Railway is not open to the general public.

Introduction

The Downs School was opened in September 1900 by Herbert William Jones who, having been Headmaster of Leighton Park School, Reading, found that his motivation lay with boys of younger age and in consequence he founded a preparatory establishment for boys on the west side of the Malvern Hills. Both he and wife were members of the Society of Friends and the School was to become a well-known Quaker establishment.

Hobbies were an important feature of the curriculum from the outset, and were a legacy of Leighton Park, their purpose being to use spare time creatively. Geoffrey Hoyland (GH herein), then a master in the Lower School at Uppingham, was appointed a Junior Partner at The Downs in January 1919 and became Headmaster in January 1920. In July 1919, he married Dorothea Cadbury, a daughter of Mr. & Mrs. George Cadbury. He was to become the founder of The Downs Light Railway (herein the DLR), the object of our story. The story is not just about the Railway but about the boys and girls involved in it, its appeal over the years, how some viewed it as the one bright star in the School's firmament while others viewed it as the enemy of an easy life.

Geoffrey Hoyland was to become well known for his innovative ideas about education and The Downs School became a sought-after establishment under his Headship. But to readers herein, his interest in practical engineering and the manner in which it was available to boys of 11 years and upwards, was his unique quality. GH was aided and abetted by his uncle, Frank Hoyland who, from the turn of the century, had built up a fine collection of stationary steam engines and railway locomotives, the latter from $2^{1}/_{2}$ ins. gauge upwards. Almost all were made in his private workshop. GH could sense an opportunity here through which his uncle, himself and the boys would derive pleasure. So began a vision of The Downs Light Railway.

It was GH who called those on the Hobby, 'Engineers' and, although the scale of their involvement was but a fraction of that today, it reflected the forward-looking methods of the

Geoffrey Hoyland was the visionary who saw that boys had much to learn from activities apart from their conventional education. He came to The Downs School in 1919 as a Junior Partner and was Headmaster from 1920 until 1940 during which time he became the founder of The Downs Light Railway.

J. Hoyland

Headmaster in the early 1930s, for which the School was becoming notable.

With boys under the age of 11 not being permitted to join, there was keen competition for a place: the 'Engineers' were something of an elite among them. On the Railway they marked out the platforms and dug the foundations. They learned quickly that a measured rectangle was subtly different from a similarly

The start of it all. The engine which Frank Hoyland bought; it became the catalyst from which The Downs Light Railway emerged. Here it is working at the Children's Welfare Exhibition, London in 1913.

Bassett-Lowke Society Collection

measured parallelogram. They found out the hard way that flipping creosote haphazardly with a brush burned the face on the one day when it was Matron's half-day off. Also, that the simple task of fitting two fishplates to a rail joint, inserting four bolts and fixing on the nuts, whilst held all together with one juvenile hand, requires at least one more hand; more frustrating still was to find the finished work had been assembled the nuts INSIDE the rails . . . . '*Quickly, undo it before Sir sees it*'.

In those pre-Second World War days there were two hobby afternoons a week. Sunday afternoons would also find us down on the Railway; they were an extra opportunity for cleaning engines, firetubes, smokeboxes, raking out fireboxes, oiling round and very occasionally, raising steam. Sometimes the boys were left to light up unsupervised, for GH preferred to spend his Sunday afternoon sitting in a deep armchair in the Study, smoking his pipe. Infrequently the goal of seeing an engine move under its own steam was reached for there were many pitfalls in the way. Perhaps the (new) electric blower was off colour, and the substitute 6 ft. of rainwater pipe stuck down the chimney of the engine, ineffective. Often there was insufficient firewood and what there was suffered damp .... even the box of matches was non-co-operative and was nearly empty. When at length a feeble flame was created, a misguided lad would throw coal on too soon and suffocate the lot! In no time at all it was teatime and we had to change into a suit for the Sunday evening service so dashing our hopes for another week. Among

one's recollections of the frenzy to see a whiff of steam rising in the air are of the boy who exceeded his brief, removed all the firebars and forgot where he had put them, so delaying things that it was too late to even begin. Then there were days when the fire was not responding to the pull on it from the blower. A mystery indeed until it was found that the smokebox door had not been fully closed!

Even when our hopes were fulfilled, it was always the seniors who monopolised the driving, and no one thought of attaching wagons so that everyone could ride. Often the engine would come off the rails as it left the turntable and the opportunity was lost once more. Then there was a final coup-de-grace: the boiler water level was too low and it was found that the injector would not work (a frequent experience). 'TUBBY' had an axle pump and water could be pumped into the boiler by pushing the engine along the line in the hope that the turning wheels would make enough revolutions to save the day. We were exhausted long before then. Nevertheless, fresh and keen to try again, we would assemble at 'WINDERMERE' on the following Sunday.

Geoffrey Hoyland was a compulsive photographer owning one of the first 35mm Leica cameras. His pictures of the hobby in the hot summers of the late 1930s show railway activities with boys naked to the waist with shorts and sandals; when the DLR was 'on show' in the Summer Term the operators might discard boiler suits for games' wear with white pullovers, short trousers, sock-less legs and sandals. In an age when children were not cosseted as they are today, the casual dress on the hobby would seem to invite burns and accidents, especially to near-bare feet. The white pullovers were beautifully warm and on the DLR they became liberally laced with soot, oil or creosote, making them partially rainproof!

As there was none other than GH who knew anything about the subject, should he be called away the hobby relied on the most senior boy. As the tasks were basically simple, this sufficed. After GH's retirement there was a tendency to engage the boys on work which was unlikely to have much effect on the Railway itself i.e. building unnecessary sidings or walls, etc. In the 1960s supervision had become so minimal that things got out of hand and certain boys took pleasure in causing derailments which would create havoc. Obviously it required several years before this attitude could be changed.

Two aspects have remained unchanged throughout the 75 year life of the DLR; firstly, that boys will be boys and secondly, that most academics see no educational value in any activity which involves 'Playing Trains' and getting your hands dirty (as they see it). It is an occupation with which they do not wish to be associated. These two aspects are undimmed by time and may drive an unfortunate pedagogue, who feels passionately that a railway opens the Gate of Learning through which every child should pass, into an early grave.

Many of our tasks are too heavy to be done by young individuals. Organised teams are arranged, if the work demands it, and potential leaders can then be recognised. Thus boys who are not outstanding in the classroom or the sports field frequently find their achievements on the DLR. Supervision is low key as a handful of boys is always capable of taking charge, and those with the necessary knowledge will pass it on to those without. Nothing is beyond our capacity especially if there is a good team leader who can shout the odds. 'Sir' often says, '*You do the lifting and I will provide the grunts*'.

Every child is a volunteer and if a child refuses to drive the steam engine he is not forced to do so, but he is expected to take his turn at driving the once-weekly work trains which do not use steam haulage. There is usually a hard core of boys who remain with the hobby for all their time at the School. We go through times when the boys can be split into groups, each with a leader. It is wise to have one boy who is in overall charge; he is usually nominated '*Superintendent of the Line*'.

Exceptionally we can find ourselves in a position where outstanding boys can be left to work alone without supervision; it has been known for up to five boys to be so capable by the time they leave for their next school. After such an exodus the hobby may be denuded of experience.

Basic training begins with learning how to effect certain movements; wagons are pushed around by hand so that the principle of pointwork is understood. Later, shunting competitions take place and the exercise is then developed to the point where the shunting is done not by hand but by learner-drivers using 'TIM', the petrol-hydraulic locomotive. Such learning was never necessary in the past when every pupil had a model railway and understood the functions of operating.

During such movements, derailments will occur with boys unused to a railway environment, which leads to the old adage, '*He who gets it off, gets it on*'. The locomotives and wagons are too heavy for young boys and girls to lift single-handed and even when using teamwork it requires an adept leader to restore the status quo. A loaded wagon or locomotive needs the aid of wooden packing and a long timber beam enabling two boys to re-rail them; a useful practical lesson in the use of levers. Wagons are given removable floors and, with the floor out, a boy can stand within the wagon and lift each wheel-set on to the rails.

Down the years safety has become a national fetish; it has never been anything else on the DLR which has had safety rules from birth. The boys are engaged on workshop practices and in operating trains which are inseparable from risk but they will be reasonably proficient by the time they are ten years old and will work with minimal supervision. However, even little railways can have quite 'big' accidents!

Incidents are always good for a laugh and some reminiscence starting, '*Do you remember when Buzz was driving and every wagon derailed?*' And the cause? The shovel fell off the engine's tender onto the track and derailed the train. On one occasion a train was crossing the facing points and entering 'HOYLAND DOWN' station with five wagons full of visitors behind the engine. The first wagon jumped off the track and brought all the following ones off too. The result was chaotic, a veritable gallimaufry. The bewildered passengers continued to sit in the now-derailed wagons. 'Sir' shouted, '*If you were the parents of the Railway boys, we would tell you this is part of their experience, an 'added extra' for which the School makes no charge*'. An unforeseen risk results when overseas children who can speak little English join the hobby as they are prey to accidents in circumstances which other children would naturally avoid. On one occasion two overseas boys were pushing two wagons full of ballast; they reached the appointed destination and the gang leader shouted '*Stop*'. Instead, they abandoned the wagons and, not understanding the instruction, turned away with the result that the wagons ran away down the hill at such speed that no one could catch them!

Today, whilst most boys have an elementary knowledge of computers they do not possess a model railway. Their computer games induce a sense that recreation is wholly achieved in the sitting position, by the pressing of keys and a fixation with the computer screen. Hence few are familiar with the fundamental features of railway operation and how to set the track for an intended train movement. Fifty years ago children found answer to such challenges in the operation of their personal model railways; today's computer games are an inadequate substitute. It is an outcome of modern living and the protective screening of children, that they have to learn how to strike a match and light the engine's fire! Thus the boy who messes about with tools, dismantles bicycles and builds up kits in his spare time has a natural place amongst us. In the workshop a boy will use the most efficient tool available. Today, gone is the drudgery involving filing, cutting, etc. which breaks the spirit of any youngster. Electric grinders, power driven hacksaws and electric drills are among the order of the day; an exclamation of delight may come from a child who has just mastered a strange aide; '*I must tell my Father to buy one of these*'.

As every new pupil drawn by enthusiasm to the Railway quickly discovers, another term for 'railway' is 'work', but he soon comes to look down upon his fellows, who scorn his achievements, as pathetic in his eyes. True, it is hard to persuade those of little faith; that is, until the day dawns when they see a steam train and acquire a sudden and irresistible urge to join those who have prior place to drive, operate and superintend the proceedings. In a flash their eyes are opened, and self-consciously, in a whisper they enquire, '*Can I have a ride?*' He or she is informed that this privilege is for the members of the Railway Hobby … except on special occasions!

It is remarkable that some boys who are looked-up-to for their prowess at cricket or rugby, never try their hand at this railway business. A lady-Head, who was made of sterner stuff,

received engine-driving tuition from an 8-year old boy, and drove the train excellently. She discovered why certain boys never crossed our threshold; '*The tunnel was terrifying; black as pitch and swirling smoke. There were red-hot coals from the chimney bouncing down off the tunnel roof, and the noise . . . to think I was doing it! I loved it*'.

A certain Headmaster, who only took prospective parents to see the Railway if they insisted upon doing so, admitted he feared such occasions as he was expected to answer the usual questions. These included: '*How often do you have it out?*', '*How fast does it go?*' or '*How long is the Railway?*' 'Sir' has model answers to these such as, in order, '*As seldom as possible; it requires a lot of effort*'. '*We are more concerned as to whether it can be stopped in a short distance*'. '*Too long; it all requires maintenance*' and this little frivolity silences most visitors. A boastful father 'who knew about these things', once commented to the Headmaster on the contents of the engine shed: '*You seem somewhat long on history and short of modernity*'. This observation floored the Headmaster for a moment but he quickly recalled a description I had used. Laying his hand reverently on the bonnet of 'TIM', the petrol-hydraulic locomotive, he replied '*But even British Rail does not own one of these*'.

This account may come as a salutary warning to all those who may be envious of 'Sir's close association with the achievements and disappointments of The Downs Light Railway. For me there have been numerous difficulties, aggravations and frustrations, coupled with the responsibility for the offspring of others. The exercise is not without its risks! Worse still, the current trend of a Nanny State role by the Government makes a railway of any size a popular target for interference and legislation. Less obvious is the siting of a railway system on a School property, and the uncertain future of any private school in these changing times.

These past thirty years have seen the partial elimination of railways in the life of the average child. The DLR has a role model by way of the main line railway line in Colwall village, but only a handful are aware of it, or where it is and almost none use it. Yet the DLR remains a versatile and practical teaching medium, whose assets are perhaps largely unappreciated. As we enter an age when road travel becomes less attractive, and railways come into their own again, the DLR will perhaps be considered with the same enthusiasm as it had seventy-five years ago.

Chapter 1

From Vision to Reality

1919 - 1930

As mentioned, Geoffrey Hoyland came back to The Downs in January 1919 and was to remain there for almost twenty years. His enthusiasm for railways immediately stamped itself upon the boys at a time when they were of prime interest to youngsters, along with the aeroplane and the wireless. Wasting no time, we can imagine Frank and Geoffrey seeking out a suitable piece of level ground for a length of railway track, in what was then the garden of The White House. They laid down a basic line to a gauge of about 5ins, to suit the largest engines at that time in Frank's collection.

This initial trial was of limited satisfaction and a move was made to a site in the field near where the present 'HOYLAND DOWN' station stands; this system had the added excitement of shallow earthworks. A photograph of March 1924 shows the demise of the aforementioned garden line with the caption, 'Pulling the Railway to pieces'.

Frank became the owner of a large tender engine of 7¼ ins. gauge named 'STANTOR' (later renamed 'TUBBY'), which he may have acquired when it was realised that all his existing engines were too small. It was of 2-6-2 wheel arrangement with a bogie tender and arrived at the School in 1923.

'STANTOR' had been built by William Spriggs of Acock's Green, Birmingham, who possessed an incomplete garden railway of 9½ ins. gauge and proposed a 4-4-2 tender engine for it. Finding the curves were only 17½ ft. radius he consulted Henry Greenly of MODELS, RAILWAYS & LOCOMOTIVES who recommended an outside-framed 2-6-2 tender engine of Colonial outlines and a reduction in gauge to 7¼ ins. This became the first engine of that gauge to be built with narrow gauge outlines. It seems that Spriggs had already ordered a 2 inch scale boiler from Goodhand for his original concept, and was therefore committed to incorporating it in the revised ideas. It is likely

that Henry Greenly was responsible for some of the drawings which appeared as a supplement to MODELS, RAILWAYS & LOCOMOTIVES in December 1912. The completed engine was ready during 1910. Greenly recommended that Spriggs should use the castings and detail of the 1½ ins. scale engine modelled on a Great Central Railway 4-6-0 built by Bassett-Lowke Ltd., which firm offered to help as construction proceeded.

The engine had outside frames with outside Joy's valve gear. The middle pair of the spokeless driving wheels were flangeless and had wider tyres for the sharp curves. The boiler under construction required lengthening and the firebox, although appearing to be of Belpaire type, was not so as the sides were straight with the box fitting to the full width of the frames. The grate was shallow and had to be constantly fed with coal to avoid a 'hole in the fire'. There was one injector. The tender incorporated rubber blocks in lieu of springs. At the School it could comfortably seat two boys side by side. No buffers were fitted while in Spriggs' possession. In his lectures GH was at pains to point out the unusual application of Joy's gear of which he clearly did not approve. His remedy for the shallow grate was to stuff the firebox full of coal.

About 1928 'STANTOR' was renamed 'TUBBY', derived from one of GH's puns. Alan Woodall was one of the earliest drivers; his nickname was 'STICK' as he was so thin. The pun on his surname was 'Toutbois' but this was beyond small boys who did not learn French. Thus 'Tubby' became easier and in due course the engine took the name, though the formality of nameplates never took shape until the late 1980s.

The School's property in those times equalled almost 100 acres of hill and dale, woodland and pasture, smallholding and games' fields. In the pleasant vale to the west of the School there falls a gentle slope towards the banks of a considerable

Here is 'STANTOR' with Mr. Spriggs and the two boys, taking a test run with the new engine on their garden railway.

W.M. Spriggs

stream, the 'Zambezi' by nickname; here was a small orchard. GH reckoned this was an ideal spot to begin a railway, hard up against the south boundary hedge. From here the track could run across the meadow in a bee-line until it reached the side of the New Road, the unadopted, rough, unmade road which served the School. Hereabouts the road headed up into the hills towards the northeast, eventually to end up in West Malvern; an occasional foolhardy motorist who used it would regret his zeal.

From the proposed starting point the Railway would fall gently until adjacent with this road. And then, as if halted by the presence of the road, suddenly swing left to avoid a confrontation. GH's intentions at this point are unclear - had he hoped to press on and perhaps cross the road on the level or even more adventurously, tunnel beneath it? Suffice to say that the sharp bend to the left would allow him to lay down a loop, rejoin the existing line and return to the starting point.

Enough of planning; so to the actual. Between 1925 and June 1927 a railway track had emerged from under the leafy overhang of the orchard and been driven unerringly down across 'The Punting Field' (a title as yet unexplained)*. GH termed this *'The Speed Section'*, an unfenced length of track especially dangerous to wandering livestock, for at that period the School kept fowls and animals on many parts of its grounds. On the assumption that there would be *'No trains today'* evidence to the contrary would be found when the train came to a stop and

*It may have been the meadow where football was played (punted).

a splatter of bloody feathers was seen adorning the front of the engine. Most of the boys quickly learned to make the engine go, but few could stop in a hurry! It was a different matter with apathetic cattle and later still, the Hoyland donkey.

Evidence of a sudden 'change of thought' here was clear as after the long straight run there came a left-hand curve which cut through an old hedge, a bridge over the 'Zambezi' and an abrupt change of gradient. (This phase of the DLR is recalled by photographs but remembered by no one).

A bold idea was created and the curve aforesaid was abandoned. By March 1928 *'professionals'* had laid the Railway on a new course and over two bridges. GH could not resist the building of a station on this new section; it had a platform each side of the single line and was prettily situated in a coppice of young trees. The station was named 'BROCK HILL HALT'. Unfortunately it was worthless, possibly the only instance of a purely decorative feature and was not typical of the man. Here a climb of 1 in 100 had begun and there was a deep cutting leading to what would be the west mouth of a curved 25yd. concrete tunnel. In later years (1973) this length became prey to all the water which came flooding down the New Road, so part of the stream was piped.

GH had held a competition among the boys for the most suitable name for the station where the Railway began; 'TUBBYTOWN' won and was submitted by Maurice Clark. Here arrangements were of the simplest. There was a concrete-faced platform (evidence of professional input) of ambitious length and the tracks terminated on a robust turntable set in a brick-lined well. Off the turntable a single line led into a shed of timber which could accommodate 'TUBBY' and some wagons. The turntable served the running line with a runround loop parallel to it. So things stood in March 1927.

The engine shed contained two tracks, probably to accommodate the newly-arrived second locomotive 'MAUD'. In it one could swing the proverbial oilcan. There were three windows of armour-plated glass (which are still in service elsewhere); this shed did duty until 1971 so was a good investment. The shed was mounted on those most excellent of foundations, a number of mainline railway sleepers. These raised the tracks inside by about ten inches off the ground. Apart from levelling the site, such was the hurry of erection that all was laid

on bare ground and in the Spring the untamed grass grew as lustily inside as out. In consequence, the odd spanner, nut or vital split pin dropped during maintenance took hours to find in the undergrowth! The whole station was finished off with white-painted picket fencing, again a reflection of the style of that time.

'TUBBYTOWN' was thus amongst the forefront of estate railways of that day, and had begun to appear in suitable monthly periodicals. The station was isolated from the School by some distance over a field. It had none of the amenities which are deemed essential to the DLR of today. There was no water or electricity. A small amount of coal for the engines was kept in assorted, battered buckets inside the shed and a small shelf held such tools as were thought to be adequate - an oilcan, firing

By May 1928, Lewis and Henry Headley had become the first drivers of 'TUBBY', seen here outside 'TUBBYTOWN' station. The boys are clean and wearing School uniform; the driver's gloves however, reveal that the engine is 'in steam'.

R.H. Webster

Above: *A rare picture of the train going nowhere .... in 1926 it was proposed to curve the line back towards Brock Hill and beyond, but the rails went no further than in the picture. 'TUBBY' would certainly not have gone much further as it was too steep.*

John Remington

Early evidence (c.1929) of the Engineers doing practical work on the newly-laid track across 'The Punting Field'; wearing their football clothes and boots, they shovel stone to ballast the track using unsuitable tools for the work. The wagons are suffering from rough usage too.

G. Hoyland

The simple terminus in 1931 under the pear tree named 'APPLEBY' (ex. 'TUBBY TOWN') with the engine shed in the distance and the new siding to the wagon shed in the foreground.

G. Hoyland

shovel and the like for the engines and the odd spade discarded by the gardeners.

There was then no such thing as a proprietary weed-killer although oil spillage did the trick. Creosote would have been better but like a drum of oil, these basic items did not seem essential to GH, who did no work on the engines himself. The

unanswered question rises yet again - who on the premises kept a watchful eye on the engines? Perhaps it was Banford, the loyal School chauffeur; there was no one else. The water supply was solved by pulling a two-wheeled bowser across the field to the station. To assist in raising steam by artificial draught, a foot-operated bellows was used; it required speedy and constant pumping to produce a feeble blast of air and its operator was often sick!

It seems as if GH realised there would be a temporary stop to progress while professionals built a tunnel under the New Road, for while he was active with his camera at any phase where the boys were involved no photographs survive to show the Railway's construction. It was as if he considered the actual building to be of less importance than to show involvement of pupils - understandable but a pity.

The rapid construction of the earthworks with their change of direction and the building of the twee station, named 'BROCK HILL HALT', pose the query, *'How deeply were the Hobby boys involved in all this?'* The answer must be *'Hardly at all'*. This is in complete contrast to DLR policy since 1970 as, steam boilers apart, participation in every aspect of railway construction and operation is practised. Cost apart, it is likely that GH was anxious to complete the track as quickly as possible for his personal interest was in the operation rather than in civil engineering. To this end he would employ local men through a nearby builder who did much work at the School at this time … the tunnel was a considerable undertaking and the cutting a daunting job. Both were beyond amateur labour. One Old Downian described the division of work; *'The professionals did it all and we boys simply tidied up after them'*.

I remember that a remarkable character could be found, dressed in what I took to be what cowboys wore, digging away in the heavy red Herefordshire clay where the east tunnel cutting would be, single-handed. My parents were looking around the School and I wandered down, having spotted a railway. The 'cowboy' was rhythmically digging but stopped when he saw me. The sun was very hot. His muddied corduroy trousers had the mandatory piece of cord tied round each leg just below the knee. He wore a Stetson hat and a colourful check shirt; to me he was the living portrayal of Buffalo Bill, as proffered by Hollywood. Only his horse was missing! Confident about his appearance, I greeted him and innocently asked if he WAS a cowboy? He told me he was but an American he was not. He

'MAUD', recently acquired, is attached to an over-full train at 'APPLEBY'. The engine is not in steam and, if it was, would be quite incapable of hauling such a train up the grade. Nevertheless, it makes an attractive scene.

G. Hoyland

'TUBBY' takes a full load of driver plus ten boys crammed into the two original wagons, across the 'Speed Section'. Of course they are running downhill; some boys will have to be off-loaded before the train struggles back.

G. Hoyland

By 1928 the rails had crossed the second Zambezi Bridge but further progress was prevented until the tunnel was complete. 'TUBBY's tender is being filled by watering can whilst the train straddles the bridge.

G. Hoyland

lived in Colwall and had spent many years accompanying Herefordshire cattle on the slow sea voyage to the States. I learned that apart from the tunnel, the earthworks were his alone.

His most impressive feature, and one I felt my eyes drawn towards, was the largest leather belt I had ever seen, securing his trousers. It was partnered by a highly coloured pair of braces that dangled uselessly from his waist by the occasional button. I was tempted to ask about this unnecessary precaution too, but good manners dissuaded me. I wanted to go on talking but then remembered my parents were looking round the School and might now be anxious. So I left him.

I had encountered my first Railway Contractor!

The tunnel was built in concrete in 1929 and it was fortuitous that the roadway above was School property, the right of way being claimed annually by its complete closure on New Year's Day. A section of the road was opened at a time and concrete poured over wooden formers, which were moved along as the work progressed. Traffic over it was light, so it was only necessary to build it of sufficient strength to carry the vehicles of the day. Today, as a precautionary measure, a notice warns drivers on the general unsuitability of the road. The tunnel is slightly curved and 25 yards in length; the loading gauge clearance inside was extremely generous for $7^1/_4$ ins. gauge and is still ample for the much larger stock which the $9^1/_2$ ins. gauge line uses today. There is no smoke-shaft; smoke must make its way out at the mouths. The rumour that drivers have to swallow their own smoke is misleading!

The floor is also of concrete and contains a 6 ins. diameter drain pipe. Unless this is kept clear, water gathers at the east mouth and escapes to the west over the floor, which is an unhappy arrangement. In wet weather water may seep down through the joints in the concrete, and small fountains squirt up from the floor. This damp place is highly desired by snakes, frogs, toads, lizards and the like. Bats may hang from the roof and rabbits crouch in dark corners. The tunnel has an environment all its own. The drivers of approaching trains must give a long warning blast on the steam whistle (or the horn of the petrol locomotive) before entering the bore for once inside the line ahead receives little daylight. The adjacent approach cuttings were dug out solely by hand!

Mention must be made of the locomotive stock at this stage, as it would have bearing on the decisions taken. As related, 'STANTOR' had been renamed 'TUBBY' and despite its powerful appearance it was prone to wheel slip and its Joy's valve gear was held to be a drawback. Things had gone from bad to worse in this department for the DLR had acquired a near-scale model of Great Western Railway appearance, a 2-6-0 named 'MAUD', which was found to be even more ineffectual than 'TUBBY'. It was more suited to a garden railway situation and with the boys piling on behind, was soon 'winded'.

How and why this near-scale model came into GH's possession is not known. It could be a deliberate opportunity to improve on the performance of 'TUBBY' or stem from the same impetuous desire in which he bought 'RANMORE' later. A model built by Neville Brindley Richards, who had served his

time at the London & North Western Railway Works at Crewe, is likely to be 'MAUD'. He became deputy Locomotive Shed Master at Bangor, North Wales, before leaving railway work. His grandfather wrote *'God bless the Prince of Wales'*.

An article with drawings featured in the LOCOMOTIVE NEWS & RAILWAY NOTES (1921 pp. 25/26) describing 'MAUD', although the model does not seem to have carried the name. It had several modifications recommended by Henry Greenly. In the early 1920s it was to be seen operating on a portable passenger-carrying track at London's 'Model Engineer Exhibition' and also found a place in Greenly's MODEL STEAM LOCOMOTIVES (p.24 and p.153). After this it disappeared from public view; Brindley meanwhile, continued his activities in

model engineering but leaves our stage. Its cylinder dimensions ($1^3/_8$ ins. bore) alone condemned it to being a weaker engine than 'TUBBY'.

To ensure that Hobby members were versed in Steam Locomotive practice, GH formed his own Mutual Improvement Class (a term much used by the railway companies at that time). On Tuesday evenings, the Hobby would assemble in The Big School to digest the workings of valve gears, boilers and fittings and the like, and at the finish there was a written exam. It was not lost on GH that physics, geometry and mathematics were thus subtly presented to those of us who had no natural taste for them!

Above: A somewhat badly weathered photograph of a line-up of DLR motive power at 'WINDERMERE' in 1931 with 'MAUD' (left) and 'TUBBY' (right). The difference in size is remarkable.

J.I.C. Boyd

Opposite: 'TUBBY' emerges from the tunnel's west mouth and is about to cross the Zambezi Bridge. This was one of a set of pictures sent to the parents of prospective pupils to emphasise the School's valuable asset.

G. Hoyland

Chapter 2
And so to 'Windermere'
1931 - 1936

While all the considerable works were going on beneath the road, a large area suited to a terminus station was under preparation where, having emerged from the tunnel, the line threaded up a long deep and curved cutting.* This section would ultimately take the course in a southerly direction to terminate a distance from the main School buildings. And so it proved to be.

The station site was almost on level ground and the plan ambitious. It was confined by a row of hen houses on the hill above on the one side and the wood shed on the other; between it and the road there was a considerable sheet of brackish water, the haunt of the School ducks. GH, never short of a title, eyed this unappetising duck pond and announced that it should be called 'WINDERMERE' and that it would give its name to the new station alongside. Now disenchanted with the name 'TUBBYTOWN', he gave it another Lakeland title, 'APPLEBY' because as he said, *'the station is overshadowed by a large pear tree'*.

The plan of 'WINDERMERE' became clearer; the platforms would be made from those useful ex-mainline railway sleepers raised by bricks to a suitable height. The adjacent hillside would be grubbed away to make space for an engine shed, wagon shed, coal bunker and turntable. The rails would stop short of the side road which led up to the School (i.e. somewhat less in distance than the Railway stretches today).

Anticipating the laying of track from the tunnel, there was an unexpected feature at the end of the line - a mainline carriage body (less wheels). This gave the appearance of a long-forgotten vehicle which had once run on a branch line to Colwall station.

It was said to have been delivered in 1928 and probably gives the clue to GH's decision to build the road tunnel and extend the line. Perhaps it was evidence of long-term planning? The carriage was one of many sold by the Great Western Railway in consequence of acquiring so many elderly vehicles at the grouping of the railways under an Act of 1923. The price was £5, delivered. It was mounted on the ubiquitous sleeper and brick foundations and in accordance with its new status, was christened 'The Company Offices' by the Headmaster. (In due course there were four such vehicles in Colwall alone!)

It was an excellent purchase but it was several years before its origins were discovered. It had once travelled the valleys of South Wales in ownership of the Rhymney Railway, being supplied in 1900 by the Gloucester Carriage & Wagon Co. Ltd. At last here was a place to set up benches, to hoard the collection of sacks which well-wishers had thrust upon us, most containing rusted dog-spikes, nuts, bolts and washers. These would have been invaluable had the nuts fitted the bolts etc. but undisturbed they became a home to mice, spiders and the like. Here were stacked no less than eighteen varieties of fishplates to join the rails together; a cache which gave us much optimism but turned out to be valueless as its donor had also discovered. Years later, when we possessed the machinery to modify these plates, they provided the material for many years of workshop practice. The powers-that-be had discovered Creosote and it was stored herein; its container was far too heavy for the boys and in places the carriage floor had been flooded with the stuff. There were many half-used tins of paint in the pigeon-holes, most with missing lids. These gave the interior that heady smell of preservative, paint, rope, sacking and that sweet odour as yet to be identified, often a dead rabbit or cat under the floor!

---

* This portion of the Railway possibly passed through a field, the scene of a battle during the Civil War and thereafter known as the 'Bloody Meadow'.

The incomplete 'WINDERMERE' terminus in the early 1930s. 'TUBBY', now rebuilt for the first time, is about to run round two of the bogie wagons built by R.H. Morse. Featured is the engine shed (extreme left edge), the former main line carriage body (left), the platforms formed from ex-main line sleepers and the inevitable bottomless bucket standing in a biscuit tin from which Brian Greaves is coaling the tender. Unsuitable pullovers and shoes continue to be the norm.

G. Hoyland

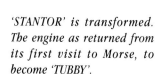

Again in the early 1930s, the camera has caught 'TUBBY' pounding a train up the field towards 'APPLEBY' in the distance. The Engineers are taking a ride, John Bowes, Gurney Vickers and James Boyd amongst them. The wearing of boiler suits must have become compulsory by this stage.

G. Hoyland

'STANTOR' is transformed. The engine as returned from its first visit to Morse, to become 'TUBBY'.

Collection: The Downs School

The carriage also brought new features to 'WINDERMERE'; water and electricity. The engine shed, dismantled and re-erected from 'APPLEBY', now had electric power and outdoor lights. A standpipe brought mains water to the site where a hosepipe could distribute it. And all these features were in situ *before* the trackwork had been finished!

The facilities at 'WINDERMERE' station were enhanced in 1933 by the acquisition of a second mainline railway carriage body which was to be sited parallel to and uphill of the existing one. It was somewhat larger than its predecessor but again of Great Western Railway origin. There was no doubt of its progeny, being a 'Pure Bred' from that Company's Swindon Works, a passenger bogie brake van of type K4, built c1890 to William Dean's design. It was 40ft. long and as a body only was carried on a low four-wheeled road trolley from Colwall station, hauled behind a steam road locomotive.

Considering that the School was full of curious boys fascinated by steam power, it is strange that I was the only one to witness the pantomime that followed. The traction engine ran up the hillside above the earlier carriage so that the engine and trolley came to a stand at right angles to it. By means of a cable wound round a drum and attached to the body by a hook, the carriage was slid off the trolley and slewed into position almost alongside its existing mate. Unluckily, the operation required a further movement to complete the exercise but somehow one end of the carriage body became stuck; the road engine driver put on steam and one end of the body reared up like a prancing horse. The driver ignored this and applied further steam. The traction engine's front end lifted off the ground and the blast from its chimney tore off the branches of overhanging trees. At this the driver shut off steam, the winch cable suddenly slackened and the carriage fell to the ground, knocking out a portion of the floor. At a later date, the carriage was lifted onto brick pillars.

Carried away by this spectacle, I realised I ought to be back in the classroom. I ran to The White House. '*Why are you late, Boyd?*' Still exhilarated, I told of the experience with breathless enthusiasm; the master listened patiently. '*Sit down*', he instructed when I had finished. And that was it. The class had listened in silence and, I thought, with considerable envy. It soon became evident that GH had good reason for buying another carriage; benching was put up along the walls and at one end a large single-cylinder horizontal steam engine was installed with a coal-fired vertical boiler, its chimney poking up through the roof. This was not all, for on the new benching about half a dozen large models of stationary engines appeared, possibly Uncle Frank's work. It would seem that GH had become possessed of all the foregoing and had had to make sudden provision for them. We were given opportunities to light up the boiler on Sunday afternoons and several risky ventures ensued!

By 1934 'WINDERMERE's development ceased. 'TUBBY' had been sent to R.H. Morse at Brighton in late 1931 for rebuilding into a more reliable machine and to exclude certain unconventional features. It emerged with a new boiler with a round-top firebox, made by the then well known maker, T. Goodhand. The cylinders were retained but the Joy gear was replaced by Stephenson's link motion between the frames and a steam brake was added, the original frames and wheel arrangement being retained. Apart from the addition of a water hand-pump, the tender was unaltered. The boiler now had a brass dome cover and Ross 'Pop' safety valves which much improved the appearance of the engine. The rebuilt engine was pictured in the THE MODEL ENGINEER for 29th December 1932.

Back again, 'TUBBY' was now in a form in which it should have given years of service but for the fact that within a few years it would be rebuilt again to a different gauge. In its new guise it was now less hazardous to drive and less likely to embarrass the driver by uncertain habits. The new boiler was more helpful to steam raising and less prone to thoughtless firing. Such things were vital to the nervous boy learning his way around the knobs and gadgets . . . . in what other school would a boy be teased because he had failed to master the steam locomotive? The writer's age had just reached double figures when he first made acquaintance with the engine in its original state. Trouble was experienced in keeping up steam pressure; inexpert firing was clearly the cause and, as to the single injector, there was evidence of occasional panic due to a low water crisis or two!

All the more puzzling was 'TUBBY's disappearance again a second time in the direction of Morse's premises - perhaps Morse had some dire influence over the Headmaster! This time there could be no excuse for further conversion and the argument put forward for it is unknown. One had to admit that on its return its appearance was splendid in dark green paint, lined

Sackcloth and ashes. This motley crew of boys, in pantomime mood, is nettle-cutting at 'WINDERMERE'. 1933.

F.M. Day

out, with a shiny brass dome. Above footplate level, the engine and tender were hardly changed but the six driving wheels had gone, and four larger ones took their place to make an 'Atlantic' wheel arrangement. It *looked* promising but was to have a disastrous effect on the performance of the locomotive. Even the most elementary engineer would doubt the intelligence behind such a backward step; 'TUBBY's future usefulness was blighted hereafter. Not withstanding this retrograde step, another was to follow!

'TUBBY' had spent quite a time away and it may be asked how, if at all, trains were hauled in those periods. The answer lay in 'MAUD', to which brief reference has been made earlier. 'MAUD' was a little lady; how GH came to know of it, and at what cost and when is not known, but it was lying at the back of the engine shed in the Autumn of 1931. It seemed very small compared with 'TUBBY' and perhaps because of this received scant attention from the Engineers. Only once did I see 'MAUD' under steam and it was a disappointing effort. Of course the senior boy on the Hobby did all the driving and made a poor showing, which surprised me as I thought he would be better at

it. The DLR was not a suitable line for the likes of 'MAUD' unless expertly driven and fired. The boys' method of driving 'TUBBY' could not be applied to this locomotive. 'TUBBY' had a reasonably large cab and the controls could be reached without bending double; with 'MAUD' it was otherwise. The cab was small and the controls packed together under its roof; it was easy to mistake the injector for the blower. So 'MAUD' languished at the back of the shed, rejected by the boys.

Exit 'MAUD'.

During the early-mid 1930s The Downs School was acquiring a reputation for academic excellence and the innovative methods employed by GH: the number of pupils was growing rapidly. The School was getting a name for itself because it possessed a passenger carrying, steam-operated estate railway '*built and run by the boys*' - or words to that effect. At a time when railways in general were in the forefront and newsworthy, when railway centenaries and higher speeds were declaimed, they held a bright picture of a century of progress in the public imagination. The

It is the Summer of 1932 and extremely hot so an exception has been made to the compulsory wearing of sun hats and boiler suits. At this period the DLR was at the peak of its 7¹/₄ inch gauge existence; apart from the two last wagons, everything was new and well-ordered but many of the boys seen here did not survive the Second War.

G. Hoyland

Downs was doing the same only on a smaller scale; prospective parents were impressed. But it was GH himself who spread the word. Often writing under the pseudonym '*Pedagogue*' he would report progress to the model engineering world in an entertaining way. Well does the writer remember a railway-minded friend who went to King Edward's School, Birmingham, saying, '*I've never forgiven my father for not sending me to The Downs*'!

A favourite medium was the weekly periodical THE MODEL ENGINEER, published every Thursday at 4d (1¹/₂p) and read by all like minds. Its weekly feature '*Shops, Shed & Road*' by 'L.B.S.C.'* dealt exclusively with miniature railways and The Downs Light Railway first appeared in this section on 20th

November 1930, along with photographs. Nor was this all. GH had made a 16mm film of the line and this was screened to the public at each annual Model Engineer Exhibition in London until the Second War. No wonder there soon became an up to eight-year waiting list for a place in the School, a situation which the threat of war only worsened. Undoubtedly the railway element was responsible for some of this . . . . . . '*Isn't that the school with a railway?*' was frequently heard.

It would seem that by the mid-1930s a plateau had been reached. Track-laying was complete and the main essentials for

* L.B.S.C. was the pen name for a former railway engineman, Lillian Lawrence (nickname 'Curly'), whose weekly article in THE MODEL ENGINEER, on the construction and maintenance of small steam locomotives, was widely followed.

In the mid-1930s, three new unpainted wagon bodies and bogies were supplied by R.H. Morse. The boys did the finishing work in the old timber shed at 'WINDERMERE'.

G. Hoyland

railway operation were available. To complete the picture two high-sided bogie open wagons were delivered (from Morse). These would be used for passengers who might sit on portable wooden seats which spanned the sides. They had simple buffers made from hard rubber blocks and enjoyed the luxury of springing. When re-gauged later on, these bogies continued to give excellent service until the early 1970s when their journals, through lack of adequate lubrication, had worn oval.

An unexpected addition was in the form of two bogie flat wagons, having a steel frame. They were sprung, with heavy cast bogie side-pieces and massive wheels; railway type buffers were fitted. Looking back, GH never made a better purchase.

Heavily rebuilt, they still carry passengers. The supplier was Parver Models Ltd. of 66a, Eastbourne Road, Birkdale, Southport.

The low wagon shed was brought over from 'APPLEBY'. A new turntable and bricked pit was sited between the engine and wagon shed, dispensing with points. The boys prepared the ground for a coal store and a water tank. A short time later the drawbacks of the wagon shed were addressed and a larger version planned; it was demolished in the 1970s, making way for an even bigger one.

GH laid down guidelines on engine-driving and good practice. *'Remember, a good fireman always keeps a feather of steam blowing through the safety valves. He does not allow steam pressure to build up needlessly so that the valves constantly blow off, so wasting steam and burning extra coal'.* Or another. *'You should become expert at operating the blower. Use it only when you need to'.* He was necessarily apprehensive about boiler explosion and went to great lengths to explain the function of the water gauge and how we must keep the water level at $^3/_4$ 'full'. 'TUBBY' had an axle-driven water pump to fill the boiler, plus an injector which we boys could not master. No one told us we were in an area of hard water and though we understood all about Giffard and his invention, together with the functions of the three cones, we did not grasp that every so often it needed to be taken to bits and cleaned out in the School vinegar.

Another complication for the driver was the by-pass valve for the axle-driven water pump; whenever the engine was moving it could be pumping water into the boiler, always assuming someone had remembered to fill the water tank in the tender! If a driver was moving and forgetful of the pump he might be reminded that it had overfilled the boiler by one of two things; there was no water level at all showing in the gauge or the engine began to throw boiling water from the chimney all over him. There was a handy little tap which when open, pumped the water straight back into the tender but, unless one checked whether the water was actually squirting back, no one could recall whether the by-pass was open or shut!

Another of GH's fetishes was what is known as 'notching up', a method of saving steam by cutting off live steam during the stroke of the piston and allowing the expansive property of it already in the cylinder to push the piston to the end of its stroke. The boys were keen to show their finesse with this feature, whose working could be detected by the informed bystander by the sounds coming from the chimney. Woe betide the boy who ignored notching up altogether and was spotted by GH on arrival at the terminus with his engine in full gear! It took some experience to acquire even a degree of proficiency in this regard.

These niceties we were expected to know and to absorb as well as Pythagoras and the temperature of Patagonia in autumn. It was testing time for an 11-year-old.

Uncertain of one's ability, yet certain of the howls of derision from our fellows if the engine came to standstill through lack steam, it was thought the best insurance against a likely calamity was to fill the boiler until the water disappeared above the top of the glass, (probably forgetting to open the bypass valve), stuff the firebox full of coal and shut the door to prevent it falling out onto one's feet. Then, turn the blower on fully, putting the reversing lever fully forward, release the handbrake and open the steam regulator. Some boys did this with panache, engaging a confident yank on the handle which resulted in a glorious slipping of wheels and a plume of hot water from the chimney! Others were cautious - their gentle handling might produce no movement at all, viz :

'What is wrong, boy?'

'I don't know, Sir'

'Look about you. What have you forgotten?'

'Er - oh - forgotten to take off the handbrake, Sir'

A peaceful summer's evening at 'APPLEBY' in 1934. The air is full of flying insects and 'TUBBY' awaits a driver.

G. Hoyland

There is much more like this but there was no shortage of willing boys. Two examples of good intentions may be recalled. It was 'Jelly' Backhouse's turn to drive. We set off from 'WINDERMERE' with confidence, down the cutting and through the tunnel into the coppice. Here 'Jelly' apparently thought he would check the water level . . . . a very tricky job on a small engine whilst bucketing along. So he stopped to make sure but did not like what he saw (whatever that was) and with GH's mandate in mind, he attempted to turn off the blower, which should not have been needed anyway. Clearly there was something of a panic for 'Jelly' was inadvertently *opening* the valve and went on turning to no effect, until suddenly there was a rush of steam and the wheel valve blew out of its body. 'Jelly' yelled and bolted off along the track, the fitting falling to the floor of the cab.

Another boy who thought he could obtain a brighter fire with the pricker (a poker in domestic terms) had a rude shock. Going along the engine slowed to a stand for some reason and he noticed the steam pressure was well down. Mystified, he was alerted to a grass fire on the track behind the train so looked inside the firebox. There was nothing to be seen except the rails and ballast. In the stirring up the fire the pricker had hooked up the firebars and dropped the bars and fire out into the meadow!

Raising steam at 'WINDERMERE' shed. The re-gauged/rebuilt 'TUBBY' is the centre of attraction. On such occasions as this the boys would argue among themselves as to whom is doing what; there are far too many of them. One casualty has got smoke in his eyes. Among the in-fighting it will be discovered that the fire has gone out, hence the 'Elephant's Trunk' in the chimney to assist combustion.

G. Hoyland

Chapter 3
Transformation and War
1937 - 1945

During 1936 GH was having a love affair; the source of his temptation clearly came through the name the School had acquired for itself 'among the fraternity'. The sequel was to have a profound effect on the DLR which, at this period, still retained the rail gauge with which it begun, namely 7¹/₄ ins., which is a recognised gauge among those operating small railways.

One can read the hand of R.H. Morse here, and the pages of THE MODEL ENGINEER. GH was to become aware that a small, yellow-painted steam locomotive named 'RANMORE' was on the market and he found it irresistible. I use the adjective 'small' for although it was the same size as 'TUBBY', it was a fine, delicate model built to a larger 'recognised' gauge, namely 9¹/₂ ins., and a scale of 2 ins. to the 1 ft. Morse was its builder (1930-31). During 1935, this engine had appeared in the MODEL RAILWAY NEWS, with a picture of its editor driving it. Its prototype was an 0-4-2 tank locomotive of the London, Brighton & South Coast Railway.

'RANMORE' spent some time on a railway at Drusilla's Old World Tea Cottage Railway at Berwick, near Lewes and next appeared at the Royal Jubilee Garden Fête of the Southern Railway in August 1935, held at Raynes Park, where it ran on a temporary track supplied by R.H. Morse and V.B. Burgoyne, its owner; the latter had had the engine re-painted in L.B.S.C. 'yellow'. Ownership then passed to Mr. Douglas Ann in 1935 then being purchased by Geoffrey Hoyland for the DLR in 1937. Its career on the DLR was nothing compared with the notoriety it first acquired. GH must have bought it for his personal delight, thinking it and a re-gauged 'TUBBY' would be all-sufficient.

In its day, this was a famous model. THE LOCOMOTIVE (January 1938 p.29) wrote, '*it has lately been attracting much attention around Malvern where it is now 'stationed' in the grounds of The Downs School . . . . a model of the present Southern Railway No. 2286 as it appeared new in 1879. Thus, the actual engine and the model are both working concurrently.*' The article continued by saying, '*the model could run at 20 mph on the straight!*' It had a superheated steel boiler with copper tubes and would '*run with a load of two grown-ups for an hour on one shovel full of coal*'. This last comment should have made it clear that it was quite unsuitable for the DLR!

'RANMORE' would have no place on the DLR owing to its different gauge but with GH'S heart set upon the engine, it had secured a place in 'WINDERMERE's engine shed by the autumn of 1937. The intention was to convert the DLR to the wider gauge of 'RANMORE', and rolling stock similarly. 'TUBBY' disappeared to Morse's (who was at this time at Woodmancote, Sussex) again for conversion and returned painted yellow to match 'RANMORE', which to the boys' eyes seemed unsuitable, it having previously been dark green. It was not a practical colour for the DLR, especially as the boys were wont to clean engines with filthy rags! The result was a hotchpotch which even 'L.B.S.C.' failed to appreciate (THE MODEL ENGINEER August 1938). The wheel arrangement remained a 4-4-2 with outside Walschaerts valve gear whilst the original small cylinders were replaced by smaller ones of 2 ins. bore x 3 ins. stroke. The tender was raised on new bogies.

Gauge conversion of the Railway took two years; many water-saturated sleepers were life-expired. It is not known how much of a part the boys took in it. Probably very little. During the upheaval 'MAUD' disappeared to a mystery destination. To go to such lengths to re-gauge a complete railway to suit one addition to its motive power fleet (rare but not unknown in the full-size railway world) would be to anticipate the incomer as

In March 1938 a visit to the School shows a re-gauged 'TUBBY' plus a short train at 'WINDERMERE', all similarly treated. Never previously had everything looked so splendid. It was all so misleading.

J.I.C. Boyd

being a wondrous piece of machinery. Pretty and delicate it was, but fit to suit the rough and tumble of the DLR it was not!

It was in early 1938 when I probed the engine shed and saw 'RANMORE' again; it was in heart-breaking condition as if hurriedly abandoned because the tea bell had sounded. The top of the cab, which it was essential to remove in order to drive, was gone entirely and some fittings were missing giving an air of misuse. The remarkable yellow livery was barely discernible. As there was no one else about I could ask no questions and it might not have been opportune so to do. It was clear that 'RANMORE' had proved a failure and was abandoned. Clearer still was the 'message' that supervision was at low ebb and a tide in the affairs of the DLR was turning against it. I closed the shed doors - why was the weak performance of 'RANMORE' not assessed before entering into all the trouble and expense? These were disturbing thoughts.

Equally dainty, Morse had provided a string of near-scale four-wheel open wagons in the form of the 10 ton coal wagons of that time. These were beautifully made and painted; some carried 'DLR' and others 'SL', the latter standing for V. Burgoyne's railway at Spring Lane, Crowthorne, Berkshire. Their running gear was a far cry from the heavy wheels etc. of the existing wagons and they were eminently suitable for a garden railway around the lawns of a country house. Their light construction was their downfall and when the boys carried ballast in them they soon disintegrated. Along with the wagons came a long-wheelbase goods brake van based on Southern Railway design. One had to sit on the roof; inside the van was a container to drop sand onto the rails to prevent engine wheel slip. It was quite ineffective, as to be of use it would have to precede the train!

To sum up, with hindsight, the final years leading to the Second War did nothing to benefit the Railway. None of the rolling stock acquired through Morse was really suited to School circumstances. The conversion to 9¹/₂ ins. gauge was certainly of benefit in terms of driver and passenger comfort (and some locomotive design aspects), but similar railways built to 7¹/₄ ins. in the present day are far more adventurous in terms of loading gauge. It was not until 1970 that the DLR began to exploit the potentials of building to narrow gauge practice on its 9¹/₂ ins. gauge track.

The foregoing comments notwithstanding in late 1938 there began one final development in the Hoyland Era, an Extension. The line was broken some way short of 'APPLEBY' terminus and a new course curved round towards The White House involving further deep and heavy cutting work into the slope. This was to be the environment of the DLR for much of its length . . . deep, wet and somewhat unstable cuttings in Hereford clay, to carry the line steeply on gradients unsuited to juvenile steam drivers!

At this juncture the prospect of war was in everyone's minds. At the same time the new Extension had reached a point west of and below the level of The White House where either a deeper cutting or tunnel was called for. A brilliant idea came in the form of a tunnel which would meet the current mood and serve as an air raid shelter if the need came. And so it was quite straight, of generous dimension and 40 yards long (36.57M). It had ventilators in the roof, blast walls at each end and was in concrete. The ground above only lightly covered the arched roof.*

The track lifted from 'APPLEBY' station was stored until the end of hostilities, and a line could then be laid along this formation, through The White House tunnel to end in the run-round loop which had previously been sited there. It was a brave attempt and gave the Railway a finishing point at each end, but the bit in-between was far from satisfactory. It was proposed to give this end of the line the name 'BROCK WOOD' after the house nearby (not then School property), but this was never carried out. This extension allowed 'APPLEBY' to be abandoned completely, though the curious may still find its concrete platform edge among the boscage. The Extension never fulfilled its purpose, though the motive for building it was sound enough; 'TUBBY' found the climb to the tunnel too steep and would slip to a standstill. Passengers had to jump out and push

the train until it reached level ground inside the tunnel bore, and then leap onto the train again in the dark! With a moderate load and a more skilful driver, 'TUBBY' was capable enough but few boys had the experience to accomplish it.

At this period the School grounds gave home to many occupants including ponies, ducks, sheep, and poultry whose numbers increased when it seemed prudent to guard against food shortages due to hostilities. It was impossible to visualise what GH had called 'The Speed Section', littered as it was with straying livestock. Before war had begun, GH had developed a liking for running a train in the dark. Several 'near misses' took

The Headmaster tries to fool us into thinking these boys are actually doing something, but even with a mattock the boy cannot lift the track whilst standing on it at the same time! This is the late 1930s near 'BROCK WOOD HALT'; the newly re-gauged line looks splendid.

G. Hoyland

* It is maintained that the local air raid sirens were only sounded twice . . . and on the same night when German aircraft bombed Birmingham and indeed dropped a bomb near the New Road!

The Geoffrey Hoyland Era is coming to an end. The huddle of boys to see the new engine 'RANMORE' has gone but a few boys ready to try their turn at driving wait patiently. The Second War will shortly begin. 'WINDERMERE' has lost the departure platform and most of the other, and a long period of hibernation is soon to begin.

G. Hoyland

A vision of neglect shows in the unkempt track at 'WINDERMERE' in 1949 creating derailments with every move. From left to right; the Morse-built brake van; a Parver-built bogie flat wagon; a Morse-built 4-wheeled open wagon; a Morse/Downs-built bogie open wagon. Each was in an appalling condition.

J.I.C. Boyd

'RANMORE' is having one of its last steam runs on the DLR before the onset of the Second War. It has stopped with a train near the foot of the 'Speed Section' while Mrs. Hoyland looks on from the road. 'RANMORE' is unlikely to prove powerful enough to haul such a train back to 'WINDERMERE'.

G. Hoyland

In late 1938 the Extension up to the second tunnel and a temporary terminus behind The White House was begun. The cutting is being dug from 'APPLEBY' but the input by the boys is very light.

G. Hoyland

place. A bicycle lamp would be hung on the smokebox door handle but was of little use as the smoke from the chimney obscured the track ahead. It was a new twist and brought added excitement.

One night, 'TUBBY', with Gurney Vickers driving, was travelling at fair speed across the meadow. He was satisfied that the livestock would be shut up for the night. The boys on the train were happy because they should have been doing 'prep'. Without warning, there was a bump, a bloodcurdling cry and clouds of steam; the engine, its headlamp dislodged, ran on, accompanied by a howl that rose and fell like a banshee. The train stopped, the errant lamp was found in the long grass and a search made for an injured beast. There was none. Then someone noticed the front cover from a cylinder was missing;

the piston had knocked it right out. The frightful noise had been due to steam escaping through the break.

After one of 'TUBBY's trips to Morse the engine had acquired a pair of Ross 'Pop' safety valves which could be manually adjusted to 'blow off' at the required pressure. In a sporting gesture, John Bowes offered to test their sensitivity for a small wager, and sat on the valves at what was presumed to be (in Parliamentary terms) a Safe Seat. The valves took immediate objection and blew off vigorously, causing John Bowes to leap off the engine. The boys crowded round as John removed his trousers to reveal two neat little rings of burnt flesh on his buttocks. They echoed the circle of small holes in the valve top exactly. In the dormitory that night this neat *'Seat of Discomfort'* was on show again; its owner was rather proud of its individuality.

Geoffrey Hoyland's retirement was sudden; he was taken ill at Easter 1940 and was ordered to take a rest for a term. He resigned on health grounds at the end of the summer term. With the start of the Second War the School had many problems and was not concerned with the Railway. Suffice to say GH's retirement marked the end of an era. His step-brother Frazer took on the mantle.

Even had there been no War (which brought shortages and restrictions of many kinds) the DLR was bound to feel immediate effect. The inspiration and creation of a railway was in the person of one man, as was the essential financial backing, and he had no successor. Important though this was, wartime circumstances alone forced the Hobby to reduce its activities for the duration. However, a plentiful supply of bagged cement was to be had and the boys were found work off the Railway. A concrete wall was built on the east side of 'WINDERMERE' on top of which a

track was laid and up which an engine could be pushed over a 'pit' for servicing. In due course a concrete wall appeared round the second turntable and a crude brick wall bounded the back of the platform. These features kept the boys on constructive assignments; they were well intentioned too. But in practice they were hopeless. It was easier to maintain an engine by siting it on the turntable. The second turntable had no 'raison d'être'. The brick walling soon crumbled. So in due course these features were objectives for a demolition exercise!

It is as well to remember that coal was in short supply and little could be spared for steaming the engines; so the much-rebuilt 'TUBBY' and the useless 'RANMORE' were confined to the 'WINDERMERE' engine shed. When an offer to buy 'RANMORE' and certain wagons came from Lawrence Redfern of Prestbury, Cheshire (a fellow Quaker), Frazer Hoyland gladly sold them in 1941 for £65. On visiting Mr. Redfern in the late 1940s, 'RANMORE' was discovered in a neglected state in a hen

'TUBBY' could be taken for a good-looking machine posed outside 'APPLEBY' in 1939 but this view shows its basic weakness; the driving wheelbase is far too short for the overall engine length. When 'JAMES BOYD' was built in the 1990s many parts from this engine were incorporated in the new design for sentiment's sake.

G. Hoyland

Above: *Gauge conversion complete, 'RANMORE' and train assemble at the unfinished 'WINDERMERE' terminus in March 1938. Note the discarded materials alongside and the 'Company Offices' (top left).*

J.I.C. Boyd

Right: *Another view of 'RANMORE' at 'WINDERMERE' in 1938 showing the unfinished and discarded 5 ins. gauge track in the background.*

G. Hoyland

Above: *Sunday afternoon was a time for leisurely tube cleaning and the general maintenance of engines. Here a boy assumes a business-like pose for the Headmaster's camera. 1939.*

G. Hoyland

Left: *Not a very good example of orderliness. A posed scene outside 'WINDERMERE' , probably just before the sale of 'RANMORE' which is on the turntable. The left hand platform has been restored but the untidy state of the station does not inspire confidence.*

Collection : H.J. Hoyland

A very good bargain for £50. The un-named 'GEORGE' in spanking external order shortly after arrival.

J.I.C. Boyd

house. It was thick with dust, hen droppings and straw. The smokebox door had been smashed in a run-away, and a saucepan lid was doing duty instead.

Wartime shortages were to persist for some years after the War ended so the master in charge of the Railway planned a major project; the Engineers would build a bridge over the line sufficient to carry farm carts. It would be placed just north of the then 'BROCK HILL HALT' in the coppice, to connect the New Road with the field below Brock Wood. There was an existing access to the field by a level crossing; even this saw but occasional use, and perhaps we may glimpse an air of desperation to find an objective for the boys. The bridge was given concrete footings to the supporting walls, substantially reinforced with old rails. The span was made of old mainline sleepers with a planked deck. It was 1970 before the useless bridge could be taken down.

According to R.H. Morse's son, Bob, a partially-built locomotive came to his father for completion from V.B. Burgoyne about 1939. The tender was already complete, together with the engine's main frames, driving wheels, etc. How these came

to exist is not known; perhaps Burgoyne's mechanic named Bell, who did work on his behalf, was involved? Whether Burgoyne took delivery of the completed job from Morse is unclear but the latter arranged the sale, on Burgoyne's behalf, to GH in 1941 for £50 including a number of 4-wheel open wagons also built by Morse. Even in 1941, £50 was a very low price. It is suggested that as Burgoyne was now associated with $10\frac{1}{4}$ ins. gauge (e.g. The Surrey Border & Camberley Railway) he had no immediate requirement for the locomotive.

Frazer must have been assured of their suitability and so the School became possessed of a 4-4-2 'Atlantic' type tender engine, ultimately becoming 'GEORGE'. Similar miniature engines were available for £450 before the Second War so it was a bargain. They found a market with owners of near-level estates etc. where an ornamental line could be laid out and where the children of large Edwardian families might share Papa's love of trains. Whether Frazer was won-over by the gift of some coal as well, is not known! The model design was one by Henry Greenly (dated May 1910) for Bassett-Lowke Ltd., and its outline was based on the Great Northern Railway prototype, very popular with model makers for at least three decades. Stephenson valve gear and a Stroudley type regulator were fitted.*

In September 1941, Burgoyne wrote to Frazer Hoyland saying that he had heard that the School had sold 'RANMORE' and certain Morse wagons. He enquired '*Do you still have the GNR 'Atlantic' I sold to your brother? I am rather keen on getting it back . . . the vehicles if possible. Would you dispose of the 'Atlantic'?*' Burgoyne wrote again in September 1942 asking if he could buy the 'Atlantic' or 'TUBBY'? He was obviously anxious to acquire them and thought that as GH had retired, they might be available. Frazer Hoyland took no action and Burgoyne died the following year.

From 1925, when the original Colwall-Malvern Wells railway tunnel was abandoned in favour of a new bore, the old bore

*Drawings of the engine appeared in MODEL RAILWAYS & LOCOMOTIVES (July 1910) and of Greenly's regulator (based on Stephenson's design) in MINIATURE STEAM LOCOMOTIVES (George Woodcock) p.75.

was left empty until the Second War. Adventurous boys occasionally spent a Sunday afternoon exploring this disused tunnel which was as black as pitch; daylight penetrated for a short distance and a pinpoint of light marked the Worcestershire end. Here and there cascades fell from the roof and coursed down the sides. This dreary place was transformed into a munitions store where sea mines were deposited alongside a new railway which ran the length of the tunnel and which, in turn, was served by a system of 2 ft. gauge light railways leading off the main bore. For many months a train-load of mines etc. left the tunnel nightly for the Clyde. When hostilities ceased the narrow gauge lines were lifted and a quantity of rails found its way to the School. Having suffered some rough treatment in the tunnel and being bent in all directions, they needed first aid before the DLR could use them. Regrettably, the necessary skill to give this was not available and the few rails which found use in sidings at 'WINDERMERE', gave rise to continued derailments. And so the War ended and we pass into 1946.

Officious boy on left to sockless boy on his right : 'You aren't pumping hard enough. Put some beef into it' . . . . . 'I am, but the water is still near the bottom of the glass and I've had enough. You pump'. *A frequent conversation when the boiler water-level has become alarmingly low and the standby pump seems inadequate to remedy things. The 'APPLEBY' track seems short of ballast. 1939.*

G. Hoyland

Chapter 4
Peacetime Problems
1946 - 1969

The track was in a desperate state by 1946. Despite this, Frazer Hoyland was anxious to see the engines in steam and especially to test 'GEORGE'. Coal was still in short supply and would remain so for some years, but luckily *'Haslam's father sent us some coal'* which allowed a limited amount of running to be done. But things were not promising; Mr. Arnold Boothroyd recollected that early in 1946 both 'TUBBY' and 'GEORGE' were out of use; the former's injectors were troublesome despite the fact that in 1941 *'the engine had been sent to L.B.S.C. for attention'*. This is highly unlikely but 'L.B.S.C.' is known to have evacuated himself from South London and was living nearby at the time; he may have inspected the engines at that opportunity.

The School Magazine confirms that both engines were inoperable in the mid-1940s including 'GEORGE' with a leaking firebox. One wonders what state the boiler etc. was in when the purchase was made? With most wooden sleepers rotten and an unsafe track, it hardly mattered! 'TUBBY's boiler required attention too. Mr. Haslam (a pupil's father and the donor of the coal) had offered to repair it, so Banford, the School chauffeur went to Haslam's Rotherham colliery in July 1946 taking 'TUBBY's boiler with him on a trailer, (thereby using some of the School's precious petrol coupons for the purpose). Despite the limited use 'TUBBY' had experienced it is probable the engine suffered from neglect through lack of experience; whatever the cause generosity found the engine with a new firebox, tubes and smokebox tubeplate; a revealing gesture despite wartime conditions. 'TUBBY' returned in November 1946.

Learning of the further difficulties which prevented locomotive testing on the dangerous track, and following an appeal sent out to all parents explaining the position, Mr. Haslam

underlined his generosity by funding a delivery of steel sleepers which would replace the wooden ones. Another parent, Mr. Simpson, arranged for them to be made by The Horsehay Co. Ltd. By 1947 the long task of fitting the steel sleepers began and was completed in July 1949 - apparently no trains ran in the late 1940s and there were years when boys joined the School and left again without ever seeing a moving train.

Although the DLR seemed to be on the threshold of a promising age, it began a time of neglect, careless handling and an absence of supervision which was to worsen until the 1970 rejuvenation. True, 'TUBBY' and 'GEORGE' were, on the face of it, unusable but the track boasted new sleepers; the lamentable state of maintenance of these engines caused the author's telephone to ring frequently for advice and a visit to the School to repair the faults. But it was an uphill task and things became more depressing. The engines were not run in the winter but were left without draining the boilers and condensate was not drained from the cylinders resulting in the pistons rusting solidly. At the writer's suggestion both engines were repaired at Messrs. Curwen & Newbury's Baydon Works at Newbury in 1949. Curwen's report on 'GEORGE' was a tale of woe, inexplicable in an engine only ten years old, but it returned in November overhauled and nicely painted in GNR livery. In July 1950, a historic event took place when both repaired engines were steamed and the DLR witnessed its first double-headed train to mark the line's resurgence. It was a cause for celebration and most of the pupils were crammed into the wagons for a ride.

To enable the aforementioned train to run, some of the jungle which overgrew the rails had to be cut back. Out of 'WINDERMERE' the going was tolerably good and some field drains were unblocked and ballast renewed. By now the rails along the new Extension from the erstwhile 'APPLEBY' into the

Boiler suits are now in vogue and sun hats are compulsory in hot weather. Two scruffy-looking boys with 'TUBBY' at 'WINDERMERE' in 1949, the engine in dirty yellow paint.

J.I.C. Boyd

tunnel (the former Air Raid Shelter) were in place, though rough and ready. Beyond the tunnel it was hoped the line could be continued along the verge of the Kitchen Garden which would have extended the Railway to ⁷/₈th mile long.

But the reality was different. The difference in altitude was considerable between the termini, and between them the line dropped to pass under the New Road. Engine drivers had to be skilled. The member of staff allocated to the Hobby had no knowledge of these things, and in fact the conception of the new Extension was marred by ignorance of the limited performance of steam locomotives hauling a heavy train on greasy rails up a gradient situated on a curve. Even with 'GEORGE' on the train, no driver could master these conditions

without resort to his passengers jumping out on the move, and pushing the ensemble into the tunnel. The whole episode gave little enthusiasm for the Extension; it was a Lost Cause! At this time the MODEL RAILWAY NEWS published two articles on the Railway, the first for over fifteen years.

These conditions being explained, the afore-mentioned account of the double-headed train of July 1950 becomes more relevant; the hobby would always contain perhaps only one boy who showed promise as an engine driver . . . . and very many who never did. Despite the many drawbacks we had two good boys, Atherton and Drawbell, who took an engine each that day. Our secret ambition was to 'charge' the abundant undergrowth on the Extension, reach the tunnel and burst out beyond it

Left: The unfinished terminus has not been the target for German bombers and 'WHITE HOUSE' station had yet to be commenced in 1948. Although a small run-round loop was created here later, this was destined to be the farthest point reached by The Extension.

R. St. Croix

Right: This was a frosty scene in December 1949 at 'WINDERMERE' following a decade of near-inactivity. 'GEORGE' appears at the engine shed door but requires attention, its boiler not yet having been drained for such weather. A spider's web of derailment-inviting track litters the ground . . . . the entire fruits of a period when the engines had expired.

J.I.C. Boyd

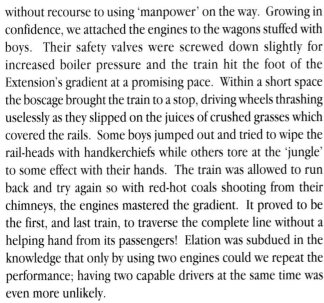

without recourse to using 'manpower' on the way. Growing in confidence, we attached the engines to the wagons stuffed with boys. Their safety valves were screwed down slightly for increased boiler pressure and the train hit the foot of the Extension's gradient at a promising pace. Within a short space the boscage brought the train to a stop, driving wheels thrashing uselessly as they slipped on the juices of crushed grasses which covered the rails. Some boys jumped out and tried to wipe the rail-heads with handkerchiefs while others tore at the 'jungle' to some effect with their hands. The train was allowed to run back and try again so with red-hot coals shooting from their chimneys, the engines mastered the gradient. It proved to be the first, and last train, to traverse the complete line without a helping hand from its passengers! Elation was subdued in the knowledge that only by using two engines could we repeat the performance; having two capable drivers at the same time was even more unlikely.

In the early 1950s the master in charge did little running, instead the Engineers were put to the task of building a long, low timber wagon shed to house the small four-wheeled wagons

which the existing shed failed to do. The new shed was in the form of a lean-to on the west side of the engine shed at 'WINDERMERE' and held two tracks with little space between them. A 'Spider's Web' of trackwork was laid in to serve the shed, mainly by the acquisition of rails etc. from the old Colwall mainline railway tunnel. Nothing would stay on the rails on this cat's cradle of unsuitable material. I decided that at the first opportunity I would bring a suitable party, experienced in these matters, to spend a week-end to remove the offending layout and relay some of it to a simple but adequate arrangement. The Northwest Area Group of the recently formed Talyllyn Railway Preservation Society (founded in 1951 to save this historic Welsh railway) obliged and there was no difficulty in finding six capable volunteers. There were ladies too, equally informed in alfresco cooking. The first affray was in June 1955, the party leaving the Northwest on Friday evening and spending two nights at the School so as to have two full days to dismantle the track at 'WINDERMERE', over which no stock could gain the running line without derailing at least twice! The working party awoke on Saturday morning to find the district hit by a monsoon and

Left: *During the Summer of 1949, with a little outside help 'TUBBY' was made workable and is seen here entering 'WINDERMERE'.*
Above: *Optimism stirred as a result so that in July 1950 an auspicious event occurred when both 'TUBBY' and 'GEORGE' were used together for the first time ever. The whole School had an opportunity to witness the DLR in action, many for the first and all for the last time as a question mark hung over the availability of both engines for almost the next two decades.*

J.I.C. Boyd

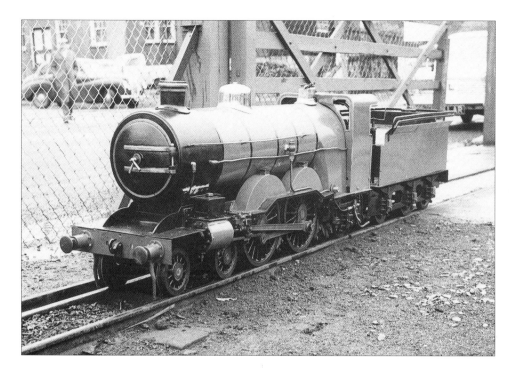

'GEORGE' . . . . as yet unnamed . . . . goes to the seaside. The engine had been overhauled by the apprentices at Wilkins & Mitchell but was sent ultimately for test on a short length of mixed-gauge track on the Fairbourne Railway, near Barmouth in mid-Wales.

Collection : late John C. Wilkins

the sidings to be removed, completely underwater. The deluge ceased and in the time remaining for the work, the offending trackwork was lifted, assessed for what might be reusable and a new arrangement laid out on the ground so as avoid sawing rails . . . . a time-consuming job. By Sunday evening 'WINDERMERE' had a simplified scheme but we were obliged to leave the fishplating to another occasion. The DLR had had a successful initial refurbishing.

Contributing towards the outcome of the weekend were the ladies who made an outdoor canteen on the platform. It had been essential that we arrived at the School with adequate anticipation of the complete absence of suitable tools on the site. In some of our vehicles there was hardly room for passengers because of crow bars, picks, shovels, electric drills, cable therein and, profiting by our Welsh experiences, waterproof clothing. A lesson we all learned was that it was impossible to remove fishplates quickly . . . . the nuts had rusted so solidly to the bolts that, even with the help of easing oil, they refused to succumb to a spanner; they were removed with hammer and cold chisel and our work took longer in consequence.

A few of us returned at a later date to find only 30% of the material was worth re-laying and that there were a dozen varieties of fishplates; 'pairing' rails and fishplates took time. There were about six assembled point units but no two alike; each required correction and two would have to be dismantled for their 'bits and pieces'. In consequence, for precisely the same reason as the contents of a toy train set box will only make one or two track formations, we were very limited in design. In the end we furnished 'WINDERMERE' with a platform line, a run-round loop and a siding off which access to the engine shed and a wagon turntable was made. This arrangement remained adequate for almost fifty years. Beside the New Road we piled 80% of what we had taken up, to be removed later by itinerant scrap merchants. The visiting party greatly enjoyed these occasions, and will remember the juvenile-length beds and that pre-breakfast school bells make no allowances for shaving time. To the boys we must have looked a motley lot at breakfast.

It was August 1956 when a similar party was able to tackle the other end of the line behind The White House. Here the unfinished Railway resembled something out of the African bush. Though cut and bleeding, stung by various insects in flight and nettles on the ground, by the evening the line was cleared and possessed a short run-round. Another section of the party persuaded 'GEORGE' to move and from the tunnel's south mouth there emerged, firstly the characteristic smell, then smoke and then 'GEORGE', liberally hung about with boscage, trailing debris, flowers, seeds and with the motion entwined with nature's clutter. At the third attempt we had given the DLR a line which could be traversed from end to end, almost free of hazard; never again would the position be reversed.

But we were wrong. There was no one resident in the School with suitable knowledge and motivation to take on the Railway though, in the world outside, it had many well-wishers. No further voluntary parties would appear and decay set in.

For a number of years I had no communication with the School which then had a Headmaster who, I presumed, had no reason to take an interest so long as the Railway was causing no trouble or expense. It came to my ear however, that the steaming of the engines had now become a non-event as no one understood the task and that both *were in need of attention*. I hit on the idea that if the boys had professional guidance we could overcome the problem. The Headmaster was agreeable to a scheme whereby he wrote to the Shedmaster at Worcester Engine Shed and asked him to recommend a retired engineman who would come to the School on summer hobby days and take charge of steaming instruction. He could also repair the small troubles that would surely arise. The man could travel to Colwall by train at Privilege Rate and the School would remunerate him suitably.

A rare view which cannot be seen again; 'GEORGE' in the incomplete 'WHITE HOUSE' station, seen in 1956 from the now abandoned tunnel.

J.I.C. Boyd

The idea bore fruit and the DLR had the benefit of a Top Link Driver for some years. But as the use of steam locomotives gradually waned, and retired drivers of suitable calibre became more rare, even this arrangement had a limited life. By 1971 the men sent had become so uninformed themselves, that we were obliged to stop it, especially as our two engines required knowledgeable attention.

At this stage Jim Brown and my brother Donald were responsible for the Hobby but the professional help they needed was absent. The matter of boiler safety had become an increasing concern, as it was now extremely difficult to obtain a thorough annual inspection. The boiler inspectors sent by the insurance company had become unfamiliar with steam boilers, which were becoming a rarity. We had a good friend in John Wilkins however, who drew the School's attention to the matter and offered to send his Boiler Inspector for the purpose. His fears were well-founded as the Inspector condemned both boilers! (John Wilkins was Chairman of a large engineering business in the West Midlands, Wilkins and Mitchell Ltd.) and owner of the Fairbourne Railway, then a 15 ins. gauge system south of the river at Barmouth. Having no children of his own, he was deeply interested in the DLR and generously paid for new boilers for both 'GEORGE' and 'TUBBY'. 'GEORGE' received one from Gower Brothers at Bedford (possibly the last one they made) and 'TUBBY' one from Thomas Goodhand of Gillingham.

In the mid-1950s Mr. Wilkins took each locomotive into his Works to be overhauled by his apprentices; they would proceed as time allowed and no firm date could be given for completion. It transpired that six years would be taken to carry out the task, in part due to Mr. Wilkins' frequent journeys overseas to secure work for his firm. During this time an anxious Headmaster would send me cryptic letters as to progress but I could do no more than explain that the work and materials were costing nothing to the School, and he must be patient. It transpired that the engines had to be taken to the Fairbourne Railway Workshops to refit the new boilers. 'TUBBY's old boiler lay on the sands there for some years, and must have been a puzzle to visitors. The engines returned by 1959. At a later date 'GEORGE' returned for further work and was steam tested on a mixed gauge track at Fairbourne.

Meanwhile the DLR was in decline from blocked drains and an encroaching jungle of brambles, weed and young trees. Neglect and disinterest were evident. The use of weed-killer would have helped but instead the boys were given domestic 'weed-grubbers' and spent the time on their knees in the ballast with such ineffectual tools. It was a penance. Around the New Road Tunnel the track was permanently under water and the interior was host to almost two feet depth of moraine silt which had been washed down into it.

Worse was inevitable. The Railway had now become a victim, described by a well-informed Governor, '*to the actions of well-meaning Headmasters*'. In simple terms, complete neglect! My brother, on whom I relied to keep me in touch with problems, had left the School to teach elsewhere. Only once a year was the Railway called upon to show its existence, namely on Commemoration Day in July when the School became a showpiece for parents and its friends in the village. For about five minutes a train was required to leave 'WINDERMERE' hauling a wagon load of Hobby boys, and disappear down-grade until out of sight in the cutting. Here it came a halt because it had run out of steam and the track was blocked by debris. By then, honour was satisfied and the visitors had continued on their way to events in the Swimming Bath, satisfied that all was well with a hobby on which their son did not participate anyway! This situation became worse as the mainline engineman, then employed, had little knowledge as to how the engine's performance could be improved. The depth of silt in the tunnel became deeper by the year. So things limped along until 1969.

The neglect and old sores persisted. The decaying Railway became a target for boys who built huts on the course, or dammed and diverted the stream along it. When an engine did actually run, they successfully derailed and damaged it; they took pride in the length of time the ground staff took to restore it onto the track. Since my brother had left the School my contact was weak, but I learned that the staff in charge were unable to keep discipline. Their talents lay elsewhere. I assumed that the restored engines were capable of use and that a minimum of attention to the track would keep things useable. When in 1970 I took up residence near the School, I was horrified to discover the extent of the neglect which in turn exposed the boys to high risks.

Donald Boyd, wearing his vintage cap, brings 'GEORGE' out of the New Road Tunnel. Summer 1956.

J.I.C. Boyd

Chapter 5
Under New Management
1970 - 1971

In 1968 the opportunity had been taken to make a clandestine visit to the Railway. The sight would have broken GH's heart for the whole line was like a battlefield, blocked by rocks, water, rubbish and bric-a-brac left by the boys on their free-time escapades. There was evidence that an occasional and well-meaning visitor had been shown round the Railway and had discerned a cry for '*Help*' rising from the shambles there. One such well-wisher explained at the time that any good effect he had wrought had been vandalised before his next visit. He said he would not come again, wished me luck, and clearly he did not expect that I would fare any better!

A change in our circumstances found us living in Colwall from early 1970 and knowing of this, the Headmaster asked me to inspect the Railway with a view to placing it in my care. For my part, I arranged to fit in my other activities as best I could for the restoration of the Railway was a challenge I could not resist, and it would be a tangible form of gratitude for all the opportunities the School had given to me. It seemed a noble cause and I was sure the School would give me its full-blooded backing.

But the School had forgotten the Railway of the Hoyland Era, its activities, his aims and ethos, and his fortunate links with the Cadburys. Separated by time and distance as I was from the School, I foolishly imagined that much of it had lived on. I should have read into the evidence of the discarded Railway that it was no longer seen as a bright jewel in the School's crown and that most of the boys saw no attraction in it, while the staff did not recognise its educational opportunities. The Second War had been a watershed too.

So I inspected everything in accordance with the Headmaster's wishes. In due course I stood outside the Headmaster's Study as in days of old, and relished it no less.

My basic message was simple; '*Close the Railway without delay and before a boy is injured; the whole system is derelict, what survives is unsafe and we are courting trouble until things are made good*'. Jim Brown's face fell in disbelief; the train had run at the Commemoration of the previous Summer, so how could the situation be as I described? Could I support my opinions?

In the face of the circumstance Jim had no alternative but to close the Railway until several improvements had taken place. Though nothing was said, I gathered the responsibility had become mine and that the remuneration in due course would be a Book Token – I still await it! At Speech Day my opinions were described to the parents as '*coming from a wealthy Old Boy who had made enough money in the Cotton Trade to return to Colwall to live*': from then on I had to live down that misleading description.

Ignorant as yet of the second and more difficult task that faced me (that was of rebuilding the ethos which had formerly surrounded the Railway so as to restore its 'Raison d'être'), I took stock of the first. The Railway which had once placed The Downs in the forefront of preparatory schools and caused its numbers to grow prodigiously in the 1920s and 1930s, was no more. Without the personality of Geoffrey Hoyland and the financial support which went with it, could anything be done? I failed to find even a lukewarm interest.

Out on the Railway itself it was impossible to find anything encouraging about it. The rails themselves, being about 70 years old, had rusted through and were collapsing and the steel sleepers, which held them to gauge, had succumbed to perpetual flood water. Clearly in the woeful state of things one had to ask if the Railway had gone beyond the point of no return? Was there anything worth recovering? The only positive outlook was to salvage what could be used again and so start afresh. I put the position to Jim Brown and mentioned that in due course we might need money: he swallowed deeply. In all the years the Railway had never needed money!

Then there was 'TUBBY' and 'GEORGE'. The master in charge of the Hobby before my arrival on the scene said he knew nothing about the subject and preferred to return to his first love, cricket! He suggested it might be diplomatic to test the engines in the company of the mainline engineman who was the most recent in the succession of retired men employed to advise the boys on locomotive matters. I went to Worcester and found the man at home; he seemed a little diffident to talk and I suspected he had found it difficult to work with precocious boys and engines in a poor state of maintenance. However, he agreed to meet me at the School. We tried 'TUBBY' first as the man said they had used both engines last year. As soon as steam was up, I asked him to drive but when the regulator was opened we were enveloped in an impressive cloud of steam! 'TUBBY' refused to budge but encouraged by the man's insistence that '*we ran last Summer*' yet knowing the state of the tunnel would prevent all but the briefest of runs, we spent some time in trying to trace the source of the trouble. The fault was traced later to the superheater returns, which had rusted or burned through inside the superheater tubes. We removed the whole superheater assembly in due course, as it did little to improve steam generation. For the time being, 'TUBBY' was confined to the back of the engine shed.

And so to testing 'GEORGE'. On this separate occasion our friend from Worcester seemed a little more outgoing now and we were encouraged when at 50lbs of steam, most of the leaking fittings had taken up. Although the engine had spent the winter without any precautions being taken, as the moments passed my optimism that we might have a workable engine grew and grew. We allowed the pressure to rise, confident that the safety valve would blow off at about 90 lbs. When 100 lbs. was reached, I realised that the valve had probably jammed! To allow more time to fiddle with it, I tried both injectors so as to fill the boiler and reduce the pressure. Neither injector would work either. We were in a classic DLR risk situation! The man reassured me that both injectors had worked '*last time*' but there was nothing for it but to shovel the fire out of the box and accept defeat. I gave the engineman his privilege fare to Colwall and back, gave him tea from the kitchen and saw him off on the train. It was the end of a promising idea which had lost its thrust as railwaymen with experience of steam locomotives became rarer. It would seem to be a small matter to attend to the injectors and if the axle-driven water pump could be restored to working order, 'GEORGE' could be steamed a second time with a chance of success.

The two injectors had never been cleaned and the water pump clack valve, whence the water entered the boiler had stuck but, once cleaned, all was well. I suspected that an earlier generation of boys had played tricks with the safety valve and it had become bent, so becoming stuck. There were also numerous fittings which dangled fetchingly from their pipework and could not be trusted. However, as the Hobby was still on 'hold' I decided it would be good for School morale to witness 'GEORGE' on trial again; it would certainly stir up some latent enthusiasm. There would be no need to broadcast the event, but I realised the risks.

Praise be the injectors behaved well; they were so good I forgot to try the axle pump. Between keeping an eye on the boys, the unlovely track, the water level in the gauge glass, the boiler pressure, and the state of the fire I was horrified to find that the safety valve had stuck again and the pressure was now 125 lbs! I managed to free the valve accompanied by an explosive jet of steam which might have been heard down in the village. Although much needed to be done before any boy could drive, the first corner had been turned.

Emboldened by the promise which 'GEORGE' seemed to hold out, but knowing that its motion and valve gear required immediate hospitalisation before any serious use could be made of the engine, I asked the Head if it could go to Severn-Lamb Ltd. in Stratford-on-Avon for treatment. I was very friendly with the owner, Peter Lamb, for whom I had obtained some business and therefore hoped for a reciprocal favour! The Headmaster agreed so long as I did not spend over £150. New bearings were fitted where needed, new springs fitted to the driving axles, Peter provided all the transport himself. This work eliminated all the 'slop' due to wear, and corrected the travel of the steam valves.

The elderly engine shed, which had been brought to 'WINDERMERE' from 'APPLEBY', was past its 'Sell-by' date and I had drawn up plans for a replacement which would serve as a workshop as well. The proposal was to build it with the existing shed *inside* so leaving the engines without disturbance. Such was the advanced decrepitude of the old shed that in fact we only had to lean on it to bring about a collapse. I spent a tiring

In June 1970, the new engine shed/ workshop under construction at 'WINDERMERE' shows evidence of fresh hope and heralds the dawn of a new era. All the timber off the old shed was used for building concrete shuttering, the new wagon shed, benches and naturally, for lighting up during steam-raising.

J.I.C. Boyd

month digging the foundations out of the hillside. Jim and Marjorie Brown generously covered the cost of the work; my plans involved brick foundations supporting a timber building with a waterproof membrane between. The builders arrived with the shed in a flat-pack state and worked with uncommon haste, so much so that, when I called to inspect the next day, the walls were up. They were rattled when I pointed out they had omitted the waterproof membrane and had to dismantle all they had achieved!

Now that the engine shed was finished I was seized by the urge to see if 'GEORGE' could be driven to the far end of the line. The track was still impassable in various places, notably the New Road Tunnel. I conjectured that the Talyllyn Railway, over which I was now frequently driving and whose condition was on a par with the DLR, had taught me that often what looked like a hopeless situation proved less trouble than first thought. So I bared the buried rail-heads in the tunnel with a shovel and trusted that the depth of water there would not put out the fire. I cleared the track of the largest rocks, etc. sufficient to pass the engine. Behind 'GEORGE's tender I coupled a wagon containing shovel, pick, crowbar and sickle plus a few tools should anything come loose on the engine. Although we had coaxed an unwilling

'GEORGE' up to The White House Tunnel in the late l950s, much vandalism had occurred since that event.

Next day 'GEORGE' was ready to go. I was in some doubt as to the driving method in the first tunnel; should it be taken cautiously to avoid derailment in the darkness there, so allowing floodwater time to put out the fire? Or should I rush it with closed eyes and unbridled optimism? I chose the latter but had to stop to restore the fire; the water was deeper than I expected but at least every wheel was still on the rails.

Though the boscage was full of brambles which slowed the engine's progress, steam pressure held up and 'GEORGE' entered the curved cutting before the second tunnel. Here the vegetation became too much and its hapless driving wheels spun round aimlessly. The noise of this together with a volcanic plume from the chimney brought the boys in The White House rushing from their desks to the windows; the School Timetable came to a halt and the spectators cheered. None had seen steam on the DLR before! Down on the Railway progress was interrupted by a pause to restore steam pressure and to brush away the verdure which wreathed the engine. It must have been a remarkable sight as the engine was surrounded by smoke and flames where the boscage had been set alight by red-hot coals

In March 1971 we built a trolley out of floor beams and this was mounted upon industrial truck wheels which could run on the engine shed track. On this we placed a short length of rail and lifted 'GEORGE' by Weston block & tackle, so that we could assess what First Aid was needed. We found the superheater header was long past its 'sell by' date.

J.I.C. Boyd

in a joyous conflagration.

'GEORGE' reached the tunnel and once inside began to gather speed in the gloom. The quickening exhaust from the chimney hitting the tunnel roof was exhilarating for soon my objective would be reached. But suddenly the engine gave an impressive leap in the dark and literally fell at my feet. In the darkness the stricken locomotive, with wheels thrashing round as it lay on its side, smoke and sparks issuing from the chimney and live coals falling out of the firehole door, was as helpless as a fallen sheep unable to rise because of the weight of rain-soaked wool on its back. I shut the regulator and pulled out the remainder of the fire to avoid any risk to the firebox. The tender had ended up at a crazy angle. There was nothing further I could do except to creep out of the tunnel, wash and present myself at lunch as if nothing had happened. There would be some explaining to do.

'Sir, we saw you going into the tunnel and waited a long time for you to come back . . . .'

The Hobby boys had a monumental exercise in re-righting 'GEORGE' again and we had a 'funereal procession' back to 'WINDERMERE', pushing all the way. Luckily no damage was done. The cause of the derailment was obvious; the tunnel had been laid in the life-expired rails which had been formed the wartime munitions tramway in the old mainline Colwall tunnel. As soon as 'GEORGE's weight had been put on them they had crushed so as to be almost flat. At least 'GEORGE', though far from perfect, had proved usable but before anything else, the track needed renewal.

A small percentage of the 1936-period steel sleepers could be used again but most were now wafer thin and the rails were an even worse problem as the debacle with 'GEORGE' had showed. They must all go. The Chairman of the Board was then David Porter, a keen supporter of the Railway and without delay he found £300 to enable us to buy new rails. It must be explained that second-hand rails were like gold and fabulously expensive. However I had a helpful contact at Messrs. White & Son of Widnes and, appreciating our educational status, they obtained a quantity of 14 lbs/yard flat-bottomed rails of standard section for us from Workington. These rails were sufficient to replace two-thirds of the existing course. The course itself had to be cleared of rubbish, water, overgrowth and the existing track. In places stonework in cutting walls needed rebuilding. There might be enough recovered sleepers to carry the new rails for half the distance. However, we still required a method of holding the rails to the sleepers (the existing system was by light steel clips which we preferred not to reuse), nuts and bolts, and finally fishplates to join the rail ends together plus suitable nuts and bolts. I dared not envisage the cost but took comfort in knowing that we should progress in stages. The cross-section of the Workington rails was greater than any predecessors and the foot of the rails was wider in consequence. The Horsehay steel sleepers which were to be taken up had four slots in each through which a bolt was

By May 1971, 'GEORGE' was in running condition; we had put a new wagon frame and body on Parver bogies and relaid and ballasted the track towards the tunnel. The first driver was Bastow, seen with Harold Hullah, the Music Master (ex Chester Cathedral), sampling the ride.

J.I.C. Boyd

passed to secure the rail clip. These slots were not suitably spaced for the new material and when some suitable/heavy clips were found a complex method of holding all the components together had to be evolved.

So we began lifting the existing track where it terminated at 'WINDERMERE' and dismantling took on fairly rapid progress, assisted by heavy hammers and cold chisels bought from the small cash allowance which each hobby received. The boys enjoyed the process but suffered many bloody knuckles! We had to obtain sufficient reusable items to assemble the new Railway from scratch; fortunately we discovered a small cache of unused steel sleepers amongst the disarray in the 'Company Offices'. From the same place came a quantity of fishplates of suitable size and a Black Country supplier sold us nuts and bolts. Before we began to lay our first trial lengths with the new rail,

we cleared the formation for about 30 yds.

When the winter set in we evolved an Assembly Line technique. We had to think in terms not of months but of years for problems were constantly changing. We still had the objective to prefabricate lengths of track, carry them to the site by wagon and then fishplate them together in situ. Straight track could be prefabricated completely on the platform, but on curved track only one rail could be held firmly to the sleepers after it was curved by a 'Jim Crow'*; the second rail required fixing down

---

*A 'Jim Crow' is a large, heavy and unwieldy apparatus for curving rails. The DLR specimen was of large proportions and quite capable of reducing a straight length of 14 lbs. rail to cork-screw shape if handled incorrectly. Two boys could set it up and a third operated a long bar to turn the screw which 'did the necessary'. After long practice the team might turn out a tolerably even result; there was keen competition between competing groups.

The Engineers at Work . . . . .

One of our first steps to eliminate drudgery was to finance electrically-driven tools; here a wire brush removes years of rust. D.I.Y.-orientated tools soon proved inadequate for our more robust needs. 1971.

J.I.C. Boyd

Above: *The unacceptable track was lifted in the 1970s and stacked against the old wagon shed. Here each section was broken down into its components; these were either put on one side for recovery in the workshop, or put out at the edge of the New Road for itinerant tinkers to collect. Here two boys bolt re-usable sleepers to the recently-delivered rails from Workington.*

Right: *1971 was a testing time for the 1930s-built wagons as we loaded their feeble capacity with granite rocks for edging the course of the Railway, and shortly their bodies were only fit for firewood. And what had happened to the buffers and coupling book/chain?*

J.I.C. Boyd

in situ to gauge. It became a slow job - very hard on the knees. It was easier when we knelt on home-made 'Prayer Mats', and bought ratchet spanners and suitable socket-sets.

The 'Company Offices' housed an amazing array of decrepit ironwork. Fishplates lay scattered over the floor like confetti, there being 18 different types. Obviously over the years well-wishers had donated what was the largest collection of oddments in the Kingdom. The Workington rails being laid required the biggest size. We only found a few so I phoned the Talyllyn Railway's Engineer and asked him to guillotine a large quantity of mild steel strip for us from which, when we could afford the necessary tools, we could make our own.

A further limitation was happily overcome when the Metalworking Hobby (then currently in limbo) became a string to my bow and I inherited the room at the back of the main School which had been built for estate maintenance. It had no heat but at least it permitted us somewhere to work after dark and in bad weather. The former Hobby had had the use of the carpentry benches which had been part of the School since it opened; this was a great improvement and we quickly discarded the syllabus of making teapot stands or pokers for the definitive job of building a railway. Though some distance from the DLR, it served us well at the time. On the debit side we had little money. We would need ballast on which to lay track and often had to suspend relaying until we could afford a lorry load. When we had funds it was a matter of priorities, of which the acquisition of suitable tools was uppermost.

During the three decades I had spent in industry in Manchester, I had made many contacts with whom I could obtain goods direct from the manufacturer at factory prices. In rural Colwall this was impossible and it took years before the Railway could benefit from its successor. For this reason our initial funds were not placed as beneficially as they might have been, but soon I acquired a 'begging approach'! I became familiar with the redundant materials lying in the local builder's yard or the obsolete stock of fixtures and fittings under the ironmonger's counter.

My appointment as School Manager by David Porter revealed a number of well-used machines that did not appear to be highly prized by the Establishment. The maintenance man did not use them and it was arranged that the DLR might 'borrow' them for the time being. Shortly they were in use in our workshop; they included a pre-1914 pillar drill, a large motorised grindstone, a

German lathe with 6 ft. capacity (unworkable) and some useful formers and bending rolls which had come via a former pupil. There was also a moderately-sized welder and a Weston block and tackle for lifting.

Cheekily I asked the Head if the Governors would allow a sum to be spent on outdoor tools and getting a favourable reply, I set off for a Mecca I had long sought, the ironmongers in Ledbury. I explained my situation to Mr. Hobbs the owner and that I needed light tools for about 15 boys and did not mind if they were second-hand. '*Come with me*', he said and led me to a disused stable at the back of the shop. '*We will take a sympathetic view of anything you find here*', he remarked. Inside the building were wheelbarrows, shovels and pickaxes, all obsolete stock. Not knowing where to start, I made a selection. Mr. Hobbs hummed and hahh'd a bit and named an all-in price. The DLR was on its way again and Hobbs's shop became our principal supplier.

The 15 boys on the Hobby overwhelmed me. Some, remembering the fun and games they had had with the previous master in charge, assumed that I was good for further larks. They soon discovered they were wrong. Shortly after the second load of granite from the Gullet Quarry at Hollybush had been dumped at the roadside, we needed to load it into a barrow, trundle it to the platform and tip it into our awful wagons . . . . which did not like it. Nor did some of the boys; the Railway had never involved 'work' before and some of the boys left us for more leisurely pursuits at this stage! '*Sir, do you really LIKE digging?*' came the question. The boys were as anxious to try the new tools as they were with a new cricket bat. The pickaxes and mattocks were especially attractive. When using these, I repeatedly warned them not to work closely together and, when a boy nearly lost an ear, I explained that as Thursdays were Matron's day off, if they required stitching I should have to do it myself, and that it was an occupation at which I did not excel! We had no further trouble.

Lying amongst the confusion in the carriage shed we found various valuable items; these included levers, tie bars, etc. connected with point construction. Our relaying had left spaces for points to be laid where required but the condition of the existing four points in the main line and about five in sidings was atrocious! I took a potentially useful load of iron in the Land Rover trailer to Tom the village blacksmith and asked him to show them tender loving care as quickly as possible. As the

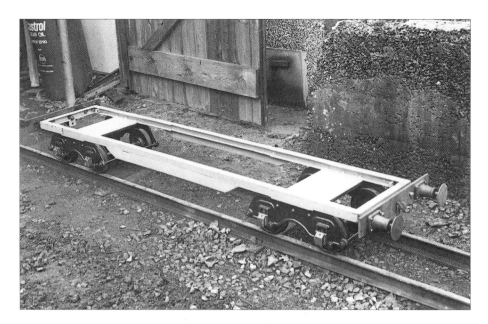

With the help of the village blacksmith, the frame of the first of the Parver-built flat wagons was replaced; a wooden open body would follow when funds permitted. A new era had begun.

J.I.C. Boyd

blacksmith in the West of England Quarry* on the Worcester Beacon, he was used to the quarry rail system and enjoyed the task.

The pre-1970 outdoor tools used by the Hobby were pathetically feeble. There was an instrument used for pulling out dog-spikes which might find its place in some museum, but the redoubtable 'Jim Crow' was about to come into its own again. Some of the indoor tools had an air of light-fingeredness about them being of the 'Heritage' period. A nice set of tired spanners was marked 'Austin' and possibly came from a past master's car tool kit. There was no doubting the origin of numerous huge spanners and oilcans marked 'GWR', which had come from Worcester locomotive shed; they were far too big to be of any

*The West of England Quarry was connected to Colwall railway station goods yard by a narrow gauge tramway worked latterly by two small steam locomotives. The quarry lay on the west slopes of the Worcester Beacon. Stone was conveyed southerly from the quarry, the tramway crossing The Wyche - West Malvern on the level. It was then taken down the face of the hill by incline to a point on the 'New Road' near the Purlieu, where the engine shed was situated.
Now steam-hauled, the course lay on the east side of the 'New Road', past The Downs School and over Walwyn Road into the north end of Colwall goods yard at a high level. Here tip wagons discharged the stone into granite bins, later to be loaded into mainline wagons beneath. Tip wagons were also unloaded on the road north of the School where a steam crane filled road steam wagons used for deliveries to customers who had no convenient mainline railway.
The presence of this tramway - closed by 1914 - is not supported by any maps, but evidence of its existence is plentiful.

use on the DLR! The big lathe had come from Southampton per an Old Downian but had been dropped during unloading so it was now furniture.

In the early 1970s the School grounds began to show evidence of their pre-war appearance. The streams were dammed again, the trees contained tree houses once more and huts appeared in the thick bushes. All a healthy sign that the boys had taken up their traditional Sunday afternoon activities. They also assumed that the site of the Railway could be commandeered for their purpose and that the Railway Hobby would gladly lend them shovels etc. from its newly acquired horde. Within weeks our stock of tools had become depleted and we were obliged to lay everything out on the platform, and with green paint and brushes, we marked everything and threatened the School appropriately. All tools were kept under lock and key in the engine shed as a result.

Did I mention painting? At this stage none took place and was not destined to do so for some time. When at length the job of painting could no longer be postponed, it was with horror I viewed the boys' attempts. *'Did you tell me that you were learning to paint in the Art Room? There is paint running up your sleeves, and in your hair; there are places on the object where you have not painted at all. Oughtn't you to be wearing spectacles, you wretched boy?'* And so on. Almost thirty years later painting is still a lottery.

Chapter 6

The New Era

1971 - 1972

By 1971 'Sir' had that gut feeling (now and then) that things were more hopeful. The stack of rails from Workington on the platform looked most business-like and, to the casual visitor, evidence that there was someone here who had noticed how they did it on the mainline. It was a kind of '*Great Expectations*' display! The feeling was enhanced by the comparative speed at which the new Railway led towards the tunnel cutting; it looked good too, on a bed of fresh ballast.

Despite their age, the old wagons appeared to like what we were doing. They ran better on the heavier rails laid to accurate gauge and without joints of a hit-and-miss tendency. All too soon the newly-found stock of unused sleepers was exhausted. We surveyed the uninspiring pile of tortured metal which we were recovering as we lifted the old sleepers and prayed for inspiration. When it came, it was a Winner. The sleepers that had passed the 'Point of No Return' were left for the gypsies. Each of the remainder, having eight rusted nuts and bolts and four rail clips still in place, had to receive a succession of powerful blows from a heavy hammer striking a cold chisel. 'Sir's record of four blows was never broken. With four sleepers each clamped in each of our four heavy vices, belaboured by four enthusiastic boys, the noise was shattering, while fragments would whiz around the workshop before coming to a forced landing. The sleepers, now down to their bare essentials, were to be drowned in a bath of hot black bitumen. Gloves and goggles became imperative and today, with all the legislation governing Health and Safety, we could not even contemplate this kind of operation.

The careful husbandry of our sleeper stock was not the full extent of our miserly ways. During the aforementioned demolition quite a number of rescued rusted nuts and bolts accumulated. By using some elderly taps and dies I could put another batch of boys onto renewing threads and thus reuse the nuts and bolts - all without cost. To justify the time they spent in 'making good' these old fitments, we explained to the boys that four new nuts and bolts per sleeper cost us 25p, or £1.25 per 18 ft. length of railway. This had a profound effect on boys who often were amply supplied with pocket money and who had never been asked to participate in cost-saving before.

By 1973 our work had reached the eastern mouth of the New Road Tunnel, albeit the last yards were mostly submerged. Inside the tunnel the water was deeper than ever and outside, alarmingly, the stone walls of the access cutting were slipping down so reducing the clearance for a passing train. We assumed that whatever field drains existed were utterly blocked. Frequent reference has been made to the tunnel; it is curved and in the middle the daylight does not penetrate. There is a concrete floor and at the period under consideration, the ballast and track was immersed in slurry which had become rock-hard. Floodwater simply ran over it. Over the weeks and with the aid of miners' lamps, the submerged track was broken at the fishplates and carried back in sections to 'WINDERMERE' on wagons; being curved it was difficult to handle in the cutting.

Back at 'WINDERMERE' we had made a 'spoon' point and temporary track over the nearby field where wagons could unload. We were conscious throughout the tedious task of clearing out the tunnel that, however promising the result, a stream of water would course over its floor to the end that our work would soon have to be done again. Some of the water came from springs which oozed out of the cutting walls. At that time we were ignorant that this is a feature of the clay-beds on the west side of the Malvern Hills and that when the water is stopped and piped away it only re-appears again nearby.

The principal offender was a faulty drain from the nearby

The appalling state of the Railway in 1972 is summed up by this view taken towards the west mouth of the New Road Tunnel. Torrents of water flow down the site of the line, its rails submerged. Debris fills the tunnel, the stone supporting walls have been vandalised for dam building; the evidence proving that the School had no idea of the Railway's value.

J.I.C. Boyd

Below: *Although there were stretches of the Railway where immediate restoration could not proceed, there were sections which permitted new track to replace the old. Here the bed of the line was raised on new ballast.*

J.I.C. Boyd

Taken in March 1972 in Brock Hill coppice, granite rocks were brought to retain the fresh ballast in place. Before wagons could reach this section they had to be pushed over the rail-less unmade road from 'WINDERMERE' station.

J.I.C. Boyd

open-air Swimming Bath, the plumbing of which dated from a period when the Bath was built. There had been flooding at a certain spot for as long as could be recalled so we dug out a soak-away and catch pit. In due time the pit filled with water in which floated many blue particles, ear-plugs, bathing caps and several unmentionables. The source was obvious. To dig up the field and check the pipework was beyond us; instead we dug beneath the Railway at the mouth of the tunnel and to our delight found the entrance to a drain beneath. The Maintenance Department willingly lent us its drain rods and sloshing about in the dark brown liquid we thrust the leading end into the drain. Meanwhile another party had dug out, found and cleared the drain's exit at the west end; with great anticipation the 'East End Party' shoved hard on the rods and, after some initial trouble, they broke through with a rush, accompanied with loud cheering. A cascade of water followed and within 15 minutes the cutting and tunnel floors were dry. We were enormously encouraged.

We must leave the Railway for a moment to return to our premises behind the School, now used as our workshop. With the help of generous parents and others, who had links with industry, we acquired materials and tools beyond our wildest dreams. For instance measuring tapes, rulers, set squares . . . . all new . . . . came from Sheffield; so much so that the full use of them required our boys' knowledge of marking-out to be far in advance of what they learned in the class-room. Then there were engineers' vices, anvils, hammers and the like; they were alleged to be 'seconds', and originated in Rotherham. The School Accountant's husband had a steel stockist's business in Hereford; a parent had a sawmill in Pershore; a friend with a foundry could let us have wheel castings; another friend in Malvern gave us a moderately-sized lathe; yet another in Redditch would turn any castings into wheels and ultimately he supplied complete bogies as a donation. So the DLR became the fortunate recipient of gifts from those who caught something of the spirit of the venture.

The existing wagons, part-made from scaffolding planks, were useless for the scale of work now undertaken; they became scaffold planks again while the remainder of the woodwork was used to light up the locomotives. Taking opportunity by the forelock, we embarked on building a set of three, what for us, were massive open bogie wagons to carry half a ton of stone ballast each (or suitably cleaned and fitted with removable seats, to carry passengers). They had channel steel underframes and were mounted on the new bogies. What excitement! Ex-Pershore timber bodies were made and fitted; a sliding door featured at one end and the floorboards could be lifted out to assist in re-railing when required. We dispensed with the vulnerable rubber buffers of yore and provided rigid steel ones of channel; these allowed the wagon to rise and fall without the buffer faces interlocking. Whilst the bogies were without springs the side-members could rise and fall by the simple system used by Frank Hornby, of model railway fame, aeons ago.

We were very proud of our first wagon. It represented a new era for the DLR and it was the first vehicle built that would stand up to heavy usage. It was built to the maximum dimensions the gauge would allow and on test the boys pronounced it *'fab'*. It had cost virtually nothing for the materials, thanks to the many generous supporters. Boldly, we risked their goodwill and asked for materials to build two more .... and got them! The second wagon was like the first but the third had removable sides and ends, and could be used as a simple flat wagon when required.

The relaying had reached the coppice where the line lay alongside and below the road. Here it was host to all the water that rushed down the road and blocked the Railway drains. The School builders, James & Co., were giving up business and we begged some very large drainpipes from them. The new track was lifted by 15 inches for 70 yards and the new pipes were placed beneath it. Their diameter was large enough for a small boy to get inside to remove any blockage! Coming out of the coppice (the site of the Ballast Platform today) we laid in a passing loop so we could run round wagons when necessary. The two points required had been salvaged from the scrap pile; their blades and crossings were re-usable but the rest was beyond hope. Among other pressing work, their rehabilitation took eighteen months to achieve and they were a curse to pass in and out of the workshop. However at the end of it all, every boy understood the principal of turnouts and the importance of a standard back-to-back measurement on all our wheelsets.

Although the Hobby had a reputation for its outdoor work in all weathers, we had various projects in mind to employ us indoors in bad weather. We had taken out the second line in the engine shed to make the repair etc. of the two engines more accessible, but it was still awkward to work on them at ground level. One instance of winter work was to raise the shed line on concrete blocks as had been done in the tunnel. Then, using some old floor joists from my former home in Cheshire, we contrived to make a trolley by mounting them on a spare set of wheels. On this was placed a short section of track. One of our pre-1970 legacies was a tubular gantry outside the engine shed on which could be slung a Weston block & tackle for lifting engines onto the trolley, thus enabling them to be worked on at waist height. And so we began a refurbishment of 'GEORGE'.

We made two bolster wagons using the spare wheels and axle-guards from the Morse wagons which were beyond repair, and these proved to be excellent for carrying rails to the relaying site, which was getting even further way from Base. Not content with this, we gave the two Parver bogie flat wagons a much-extended frame to give us two modest passenger wagons, albeit customers had to sit on the floor. These wagons were transformed again later.

We were alerted to Malvern Link where a *'large green engine'* was on display in a motor showroom. I lost no time to visit and was greeted by the salesman as if intending to buy it; *'last one remaining'*, *'Any test you like, Sir'*, was his style. He clearly knew little about the engine which I took my time to inspect. Asking if it had a current boiler certificate he admitted that he did not know but invited me to make what inner inspection I could. I opened the smokebox door to see the tubeplate and the salesman gave a shout of delight, *'Now I can see you ARE a Railwayman, Sir. We have spent hours trying to open that door'*!

It transpired that the owner of the premises was a prominent local businessman who had a large house with a $10^{1}/_{4}$ inch gauge track running around a moderate estate. We made contact and he visited the DLR. Next Spring I had an unexpected phone call from him, *'We are fixing a Saturday date for the next Conservative Garden Fête here. We would like you to come and drive one of two trains that day'*. I suggested a certain Saturday. *'Excellent; then that will be the date of the Fête'*. In the following Autumn, the Hobby was invited to spend a day on his Railway. It was an eye-opener for the boys to drive quite a different railway within twenty minutes of the School. (Unfortunately our benefactor has now passed on, and his property is now a housing estate).

In mid-Summer 1972, Peter Lamb of Severn-Lamb Ltd. of Stratford-on-Avon, who had a close relationship with the DLR, telephoned. He asked if they could use the DLR for testing a locomotive, whose elderly owner would come and see it before it was shipped out to his home in Bermuda. I explained our re-furbished line was still unfinished but they were welcome to use what we had. The engine was a large 'Pacific' type and made our locomotives look very small. During test it would barely clear the tunnel walls but we had a great day. The boys again encountered something new but they failed to match the enthusiasm of the new owner who was jumping up and down in sheer delight.

This visiting locomotive, named 'PRINCE', originated as one of four sets of castings made for the Motor Gear & Engineering Co. in 1947. The castings were based on a locomotive 'THE EMPRESS', then operating on a miniature railway at Danson Park, Kent. Ronald C. Hammett became the owner of the railway. He arranged to incorporate one set of castings, and one of a number of suitable boilers then in existence, into a new locomotive to mark his retirement. He was going to live in Bermuda and take

the engine with him. Severn-Lamb Ltd. was commissioned to do this work although some construction may have already been done at Motor Gear. The cylinders were 4" dia. x 6" stroke and its weight in working order was $1\frac{1}{4}$ tons. Hammett died in Bermuda before the engine had done much work there and it returned to England in due course.

By now it was beginning to dawn on the hobby boys that we had no money to solve our immediate needs. We had enthusiasm and this was channelled into collective thinking to the extent that everything we needed could only be obtained through our own efforts. This kind of thinking was inbred in the children of the 1920s (including myself) who expected nothing if there was no ready money to buy and were told, at least in our house, that if you wanted something urgently, you made it yourself.

It was the testing of Mr. Hammett's large 'Pacific' engine on the DLR in July 1972 which gave birth to our dream of a Big Engine Policy. 'GEORGE' (right) is dominated by the visitor! It was a shame that the track in the tunnel was still blocked with debris, and the 'Pacific' was unable to run further.

J.I.C. Boyd

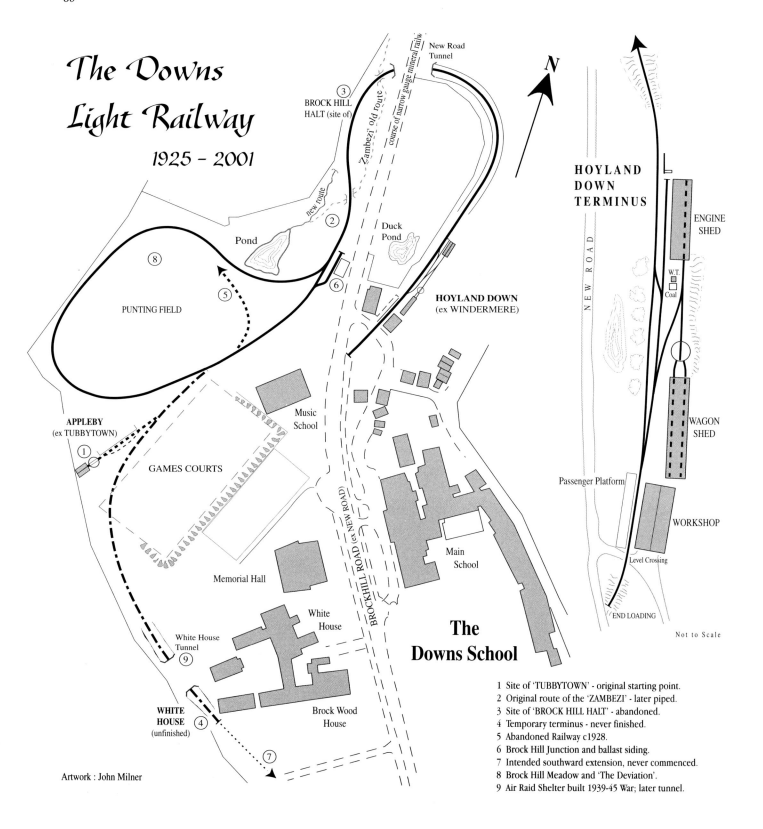

The Downs Light Railway
1925 – 2001

N

BROCK HILL HALT (site of)

'Zambezi' old route

course of narrow gauge mineral railw

New Road Tunnel

new route

Pond

Duck Pond

PUNTING FIELD

HOYLAND DOWN
(ex WINDERMERE)

HOYLAND DOWN TERMINUS

N E W   R O A D

ENGINE SHED

W.T.

Coal

WAGON SHED

Passenger Platform

WORKSHOP

Level Crossing

END LOADING

Not to Scale

APPLEBY
(ex TUBBYTOWN)

GAMES COURTS

Music School

Main School

The Downs School

Memorial Hall

White House

BROCKHILL ROAD (ex NEW ROAD)

White House Tunnel

Brock Wood House

WHITE HOUSE
(unfinished)

Artwork : John Milner

1 Site of 'TUBBYTOWN' - original starting point.
2 Original route of the 'ZAMBEZI' - later piped.
3 Site of 'BROCK HILL HALT' - abandoned.
4 Temporary terminus - never finished.
5 Abandoned Railway c1928.
6 Brock Hill Junction and ballast siding.
7 Intended southward extension, never commenced.
8 Brock Hill Meadow and 'The Deviation'.
9 Air Raid Shelter built 1939-45 War; later tunnel.

Chapter 7

The 'Big Engine' Policy

1973 - 1974

It was the trial run of the massive 'Pacific' type engine destined for shipment which concentrated 'Sir's thoughts as to how large a locomotive could pass through the New Road Tunnel? He might have been seen disappearing into the bore with pencil, notebook and measuring tape but his thoughts and the results he kept to himself. The more he thought about 'TUBBY' and 'GEORGE' languishing in the DLR engine shed, the more he realised that they were each a 'hopeless case', for what the DLR really required was a 'Big Engine'. Of course, it was only a pipe-dream; there was no money and equally difficult, the two existing engines were surrounded with sentiment and to involve their disposal was unthinkable. 'Sir' dismissed these flights of fantasy. The trouble was that such thoughts insisted on returning. If only we possessed one or two reliable steam engines designed specially for the problems of the DLR. If only we had a large internal combustion locomotive, petrol or diesel engine driven, we could run trains at short notice and the boys could learn quickly on it without the complications of a steam machine.

The Summer of 1973 saw the new track crossing Brock Meadow's Speed Section and approaching a curve whereby the original route to 'APPLEBY' was by-passed and the line led through the cutting up to The White House Tunnel. Although the remainder of the track still required complete renewal, we decided to lay a temporary line in the tunnel and, on a fiercely hot weekend, another party from the Talyllyn Railway put down the final length, incorporating a short run-round loop. So it was that in July 1973 the DLR was a reasonable railway from 'WINDERMERE' to its 1940 objective - it had only taken 33 years! About ³/₅ths. of the distance was now in refurbished track and the remainder was untouched, but could support a train. Courageously, we took 'GEORGE' to the far end of the line, having in mind the catastrophes of earlier attempts. We looked

ambitiously at the field beyond; it posed no problems in terms of earthworks and would give us a straight and level run such as the Railway had never enjoyed.

With brighter things in prospect a pronouncement by the Headmaster came as a bombshell. Brock Meadow was to be converted into a Hard Playing Area during the forthcoming holiday; on that part of the work where the Railway would be an obstruction it must be removed at once as the builders were expected at any time. I asked the Head what provision he had made for the DLR and was told, '*None. You can easily take it up and put it near the Swimming Bath*'. From a long-serving member of staff whom I thought to be a loyal supporter of the Railway, this fatuous answer flabbergasted me; in all the years at the School he had learned nothing about the Hobby. I broke the news to the boys with as much light-heartedness as I could summon. They were devastated but I assured them that, before the next term started, I would have an alternative idea up my sleeve. I was bitter and the boys had lost faith in me, blamed the Headmaster and inferred that next term the LAST Hobby they would choose would be the Railway. For me, it brought about the first step I would be forced to take to ensure a future for the DLR.

The plateau for the Area was finished within a week, so that with its extent being known, I saw it might be possible to take a railway by falling gradient on a ledge cut in the west side of the plateau. We could then link up the existing end of line in the coppice by an easy course, curve a new line in a U-turn round the foot of Brock Meadow and proceed northwards by a reverse curve to rejoin the starting point of the new line. It was dubbed, '*The Deviation*'. The idea involved considerable embankments, some lengthy curves and gradients unconsidered up to now. Knowing how slowly the boys achieved earthworks, I estimated

Looking down from the west mouth of the tunnel it is hard to believe that this is the same site pictured previously a year ago. The erstwhile 'Zambezi' is now piped below ground and the cutting walls are being restored.

J.I.C. Boyd

In the opposite direction to the previous scene, a Phoenix-like transformation is taking place; it is slow work but the oldest labourer is not yet thirteen years of age. A specimen of our wagon fleet reveals the need for a wagon-building programme for which we had no money.

J.I.C. Boyd

it might take twenty years and even then it would not be perfect. It did, and it was not! There were but twenty days to dig sufficient of the new formation to infer to the incoming Headmaster that the work had received official blessing and had been carried on for some time. The ruse succeeded.

One of my neighbours was a retired engineer who owned a well-known tool making business. Discussing the needs of the DLR one day I mentioned how useful an internal combustion locomotive would be. Between us, using a lawn-mower engine, we contrived a simple machine carried on four Morse wagon wheels, the main components being of timber. The drive from the engine was via belting and pulley wheels but it would of course, only run in one direction and we had to lift it from the track and reverse it to run in the other direction. It went like the proverbial scalded cat but its performance was limited to one loaded wagon beyond which the belt drive slipped. However, to reach a remote part of the line quickly, to fetch a forgotten spanner or a fresh supply of fishplates, it saved any supervisor a great deal of time and energy. It served for about three years until the engine was needed back again and we never gave it a name.

Initially I worked on The Deviation alone and dug the appearance of a formation that would support the Railway in a long course, falling towards the end of School property at the southwest edge of Brock Meadow. That August was hot and gave me much time on the negative side, to consider how badly the Railway had been treated, and on a positive plane, the design of a new steam locomotive.

Where, at the south edge of the coppice, the old route to

An early Summer gang completes the trackwork which the working party from the Talyllyn Railway Preservation Society had left unfinished at 'WHITE HOUSE'. Note the time-expired wagon. 1973.

J.I.C. Boyd

A historic picture: the last train over The Punting Field before the track was lifted in the Summer of 1974. The unfinished station and tunnel in the previous view had to be abandoned in consequence.

J.I.C. Boyd

Right: *Ignorant that this was one of the last trains to use the old route, a train-load descends towards the New Road Tunnel. June 1974.*

J.I.C Boyd

Below left: *Steam raising the slow way without any fan-assisted draught.*

J.I.C Boyd

Below : *The engine shed with its lifting gantry and the track lifted on blocks to ease maintenance of the locomotives. In the background can be seen the wagon shed and behind it the 'Company Offices'.*

J.I.C. Boyd

The White House Tunnel (to be shortly shorn of all track) and The Deviation began, we retained a few yards of the original route. A small shunting yard was made here and we loaded the material deposited there by various school contractors and, as The Deviation progressed, transported this useful fill to begin an embankment which would have to carry the track at about 5 ft. above and around the foot of Brock Meadow. In due course we had railed the material, moving a temporary line nearer and nearer to the road to facilitate loading wagons. Finally we cleared the site, all except for a single siding against which we made a high level loading platform out of mainline sleepers. Road lorries could now tip ballast direct onto the platform from which we could shovel it into our wagons below. Small boys attracted by this high pile of stones were warned off in the knowledge that each stone had cost us 5p. (the stones were a too-ready source of material to throw into the duck pond!)

The earthwork at the south of Brock Meadow came to an end because the last of the Workington rails had been laid down and it was difficult to see where a source of similar weight could be obtained, let alone how we could pay for it! It was obvious that we must call a temporary halt and draw breath until the time was again ripe to proceed. Meanwhile we laid in a temporary terminus where the new rail ended. At 'WINDERMERE' we removed all trace of the old terminal features and built a level crossing over the road which served the kitchens. On the far side of the crossing there was another of the concrete-based wartime creations, where a concrete-walled turntable pit had been installed. The turntable itself had rotted away, so the walls were demolished and the considerable pit was filled in with ballast. By ending the line here, we obtained another train length of railway.

On a weekend visit in 1951 I had walked up the narrow gauge quarry railway on Clee Hill, east of Ludlow and found their small locomotive, disused and derailed, on the hillside.

The first train to traverse a section of the incomplete Deviation ran in July 1975. A shelf was cut into the slope below the newly-built games' pitch and further opportunities taken in favour of the railway's new route to relieve it of the impasse created by the loss of its original course. John Coughtrie is senior driver.

J.I.C. Boyd

The design had much to commend it and I made a suitable drawing. I explained my ideas to David Curwen, a miniature locomotive builder, whom I had met through David's cousin Tom Rolt whilst working as a volunteer on the Talyllyn Railway. Thus, a small hamlet near Devizes was to be the birthplace of the first locomotive in our Big Engine policy, the first fruits of 'thinking big'.

The idea was to replace 'TUBBY' and 'GEORGE' with a simple tender locomotive the design of which would be centred on a four-wheeled plan, so that all wheels would be available for adhesion, and its loading gauge would be the largest possible to clear the tunnel. Thus with only four wheels to each vehicle, it would be possible for the boys alone to re-rail it after an accident. To increase adhesion the engine would have side tanks and there would be an additional water tank in the tender. It would have outside frames, Hackworth (or similar) valve gear, and Hall cranks. Most importantly, it had to be cheap!

David agreed to the principle of a robust four-coupled locomotive with a four-wheeled tender, the length of each to be suited to transporting them, side by side, in my trusty ex-Army trailer. It had to be heavily built, of a maximum size to enable two boys to sit side-by-side in the cab and all the fittings, in order to simplify maintenance, had to be available over a retail counter. The first component was a steam hooter from a Foster traction engine that 'Sir' had discovered being scrapped in Preston Docks years before. Slowly David Curwen and his brother-in-law began the new locomotive, which I had decided would be named 'BROCK' after the School logo. For some years 'Sir' made visits to see the engine under construction. It filled the maker's small workshop and for some processes had to be stood on end!

As we had removed the second track in the engine shed, the arrival of 'BROCK' would be an embarrassment in terms of housing it, as witnessed by a sign over the shed doors reading, 'NO VACANCIES'! Restoring the second track in the shed would create more problems than it solved but a recent visit to one of Portugal's main termini had given me an idea. Here, due to lack of space, the engines of train arrivals were released by means of traverser whereby a locomotive and tender could be

The 'Big Engine' policy comes to fruition. 'BROCK' in an advanced state of construction, at David Curwen's Works.

J.I.C. Boyd

moved sideways onto an adjoining track. The necessary and similar piece of equipment would be almost 10 ft. long to accommodate 'Sir's second 'Big Engine', should it ever come into being. To build this ourselves would involve the largest piece of engineering to date and a challenge too good to miss. We removed a section of track and placed the traverser into the resultant gap, which enabled a vehicle on it to be moved sideways out of the way. The traverser had four large flanged wheels running on rails set into the floor. Finally a suitable length of plain track was dropped back into the space in the line from which it came. Thus, the shed could eventually accommodate two steam and one internal-combustion locomotive.

This exercise turned our minds to the matter of a turntable; we could move an engine sideways now, but not turn it round.

There used to be a nice well-type turntable in front of 'WINDERMERE' engine shed in 1930 which had brick walling but, when I returned to the School in 1970, there was no trace of it. Not only did it select the lines in the engine shed, it did the same for the wagon shed opposite and was thus a multi-purpose facility saving the use of four points.

We designed a replacement wagon shed with concrete block lower walls, timber uppers, corrugated iron sheeting. The roof and doors were made from gates kindly donated by one of the staff at Lloyds Bank in Colwall. Purposely we made the shed as long as the site would allow. It had a back door through which one track could be extended. The outdoor tools, drums of creosote and the like soon filled up the spare space. All too soon the shed became a nesting place for birds and mice; rabbits found it an excellent place in which to breed. The boys, intrigued by strange smells from within, would find the decomposing corpses of baby rabbits, field mice or fledglings on the floor where owls, cats or foxes had found a way in.

This was the first building work in which the boys had been engaged and the mixing of concrete, ladder-work up on the roof and the setting of concrete blocks was greatly enjoyed. And there came a lucky bonus. We were levelling the ballast outside the doors in order to install a parallel point for the two tracks, when a boy's pick struck a blue engineering brick. Investigating further, we found it to be part of the curved brick wall of the original turntable pit which 'Sir' had helped to build in the 1930s. The brickwork was in poor condition and we had it professionally rebuilt. At the same time a useful contact gave us a generous length of field drain. We dug a deep trench from the turntable into the adjoining field and coining the vernacular of the day the boys dubbed it, 'One of the Great Little Drains of Colwall'. Actually, it is largely ineffectual, as the water table hereabouts is too high.

By using the newly-found turntable pit, we could use the table instead of the valuable point we intended to install and could thus use it elsewhere. Exciting though the discovery and rebirth of the original table well was, a measuring session showed that the 1930s turntable was only long enough to turn 'GEORGE', our biggest engine. The diameter of the pit prevented anything longer than this but it would be possible for the replacement rails it carried to have a short overhang and so increase the length by about 9 ins. Many years later, when the third 'Big Engine' came into being, we had to cantilever extension rails on each

In January 1984, an attempt was made to improve the drainage in the turntable pit with a length of perforated agricultural piping given to us by a well-wisher. The hobby enjoyed digging the trench to receive it but the exercise has not been successful, as the water-table is too high.

J.I.C. Boyd

end to accept the length of 'JAMES BOYD'.

One day a parent sidled up to 'Sir' and asked if we could use some steel? I took him down to the unfinished turntable pit and pointed to the non-existent table. *'If we could have two steel joists for the table, we could avoid making them in wood'*, 'Sir' said. Two joists duly arrived, plus many other useful bits and pieces. There was no invoice and we were very grateful. Our good fortune did not end there. A boy fell over a nasty, upright steel bar in the pit. It was the original centre pin round which the table revolved, still sound and as good as the day it was put in.

We now caught the *'Engineering Bug'*! As the massive structure of the table took shape, the fever to find an excuse to build a steel structure akin to the Forth Bridge had to be suppressed. The Headmaster caught the mood and made regular visits to admire our progress. The ghastly turmoil in the 'Company Offices' turned up trumps again when it surrendered four excellent rollers suitable to our needs and the blacksmith in Barnards Green (Tom Stephens had now retired) made us a nice circle of rails for the pit. 'Sir's neighbour, equally delighted with achievement, made a date plate for us to put in place.

All the foregoing took place during Christopher Syers-Gibson's headship, who showed much of that same enthusiasm as GH had done in former days. On hearing the engine whistle from his Study, he would sneak down to the Railway. *'Anyone about?'*, he would exclaim in subdued tones, *'Can I have a drive?'*

'Sir's plan was to bring The Deviation on a right hand curve down to the level of Brock Meadow playing field. This curve would carry the line through 180 degrees to enable it to proceed from the lowest point on the Railway, and up along the western boundary. The route would have to drop 6ft. from its present end to the lowest point, and all of it on a curve. The curve would have to be made as generous as possible to accommodate 'Sir's notional 'Big Engine'. An embankment had to be created to carry the Railway along this section which would employ the Hobby for years. 'Sir' kept those problems to himself.

During the next School holidays, armed with wooden pegs and a hammer, 'Sir' might be seen driving pegs into the rugby field below the end of the line on a *'By guess and By God'* basis! Nothing could persuade him that the proposal was sane but nothing would prevent the rugby ground from being foreshortened slightly to accommodate the route. With the conclusion that the Hobby boys (and now we had girls as well) would enjoy the project as much as he would, 'Sir's mind was made up. From some as yet unknown source they would tip wagon-loads of material from the end of the existing track and, using redundant track, a rough and temporary line would creep forward over the newly-tipped formation. To acquire materials, we laid a rough siding near the New Road and commenced an earth quarry there. Additionally we scoured the School's rubbish for anything suitable. Rocks, bricks, old washbasins and lavatory pans took their share. Then we heard that British Rail was demolishing Malvern Link station, and arranged for it to be tipped suitably near the DLR. Builders in the district followed suit. Soon the earthworks had buried 'Sir's secrets. Such is the rapacious appetite of civil engineering that The Deviation still requires attention where subsidence has occurred.

'Sir's other secret was in advanced condition; he must learn the road to Devizes!

Artwork by former pupil, Stephem Wallace Age 12

Chapter 8

Some Gains – Some Losses

1975 - 1984

It was decided to mark the 50th anniversary of the DLR suitably. Luckily, the former Headmaster Frazer Hoyland and his wife were over from their home in New Zealand and it was he who, with school flag flying and brass band playing, drove the commemorative train which burst through a tape of red and green, to enter the newly-named 'HOYLAND DOWN' station (formerly 'WINDERMERE'). To the sharp-eyed the event was surrounded by evidence of the improvements in hand. There were lengths of steel to complete the turntable and to add further wagons to our fleet. The crumbling brick walls which backed the platform were under demolition.

About this time, 'Sir' received a phone call to say that 'BROCK' was ready and, with his Land Rover and a local farmer's stock trailer, he set off for Devizes. Before starting the return journey, 'BROCK' was given a steam test and then run up an inclined track into the covered trailer. Stopping at a nearby garage for petrol the attendant (those were the days before self-service), noticing a slight whiff of steam issuing from the trailer, remarked; *'The beast in there seems to be very angry'*. I let him look inside; his expression said it all!

The boys were itching to try out 'BROCK' but having experience 'Sir' knew that initially we might expect teething troubles which could not be overcome immediately. He chose one or two boys to assist him. Difficulties encountered concerned the size of the firebox, the lack of steaming space, constant priming, injector failure, valve gear defects . . . . any one alone would have dissipated our high hopes. However, it was to be twelve years before all these defects would be rectified but meanwhile the engine was used to the best of its potential. Ultimately it fulfilled 'Sir's vision excellently.

Despite the drawbacks of 'BROCK', we could not resist the occasion when 'TUBBY', 'GEORGE' and 'BROCK' could be

steamed all at the same time. The boys then on the hobby had never experienced having more than one engine running on a single line and we had to school them well in advance on the dangers involved. This enabled us to introduce them to 'Token Working' whereby an accepted 'token' gives an engine driver authority to run on a specified section of single line appropriate to that token. The boys quickly took up this added dimension to operating a safe railway. Perhaps the vision of two steam trains meeting head-on in the tunnel was very vivid! Token Working is now the accepted pattern and it has been further enhanced.

Despite our good luck in finding enough earth etc. to prosecute the embankment at the far end of Brock Meadow, a load from such old wagons as we could use for such muck-shifting, duly tipped over the end of the line, hardly made any difference. The wet and heavy clay was hard going for the boys and the news that our good friends at Alan Keef Ltd. had some suitable second-hand rails for us, was received with acclamation. Now we could lay a 'permanent way' along the top of our hard work.

Some months apart, Keef delivered the anticipated rails. The first batch was from Butlin's abandoned Holiday Camp miniature railway at Filey and the second came from his railway at Minehead; all complete with fishplates too. The Filey consignment went into extending the line without delay but the Minehead rails were not such a good bargain as they were somewhat corroded by sea-water; the latter system had been laid in (roughly) a large circle so many of the rails were curved and first of all had to be straightened out.

We decided to extend the rails even though the unfinished embankment was not up to its intended height. The roughly laid track was lifted up on pillars of concrete blocks and the

DOWNS LT. RAILWAY
❀ FREE PASS ❀
GOLDEN JUBILEE
1925 - 1975

Golden Jubilee . . . .

1925 - 1975

It is the 50th Anniversary of the DLR in September 1975 and the local newspaper has suddenly realised that there is a newsworthy item right under its nose. So we waste a whole afternoon posing for pictures in unsuitable attitudes. Here is the nicest of them; we may thank such boys as these for the fine railway it has become in the New Millennium.

Berrow's Newspapers

The DLR owes much to Talyllyn Railway Preservation Society members. On a special day in October 1975 their members have the DLR to themselves. Locomotives are (left to right) 'GEORGE', 'TUBBY' and 'BROCK'.

J.I.C. Boyd

A load of young ladies is run for the Commemoration celebrations, July 1975. Their behaviour was much better that day than that of the new engine 'BROCK', which was disappointing.

J.I.C. Boyd

The building of 'HOYLAND DOWN' turntable in December 1975 was one of the first major engineering jobs undertaken. Enthusiastic parents gave the bricks, steel and timber. In the wet winters of Colwall the flooded pit becomes a haven for frogs, newts and toads, the subject of timely Rescue Missions and the cause of water-filled Wellington Boots!

J.I.C. Boyd

rubble-filled wagons were end-unloaded and so brought the formation-level up beneath it. Although something akin to the Alps, the whole was then lifted up in stages by placing further blocks on top of the pillars; though unsuitable to carry the weight of locomotives, progress was accelerated and enthusiasm burned brightly. Our own workshop then produced three stout wagons; two had lift-out end doors and the third could be converted into a flat wagon as ends and sides could be removed allowing the contents a 'quick exit'.

Although the intervening railway was of a rough order, we brought the track by an ever-diminishing earthwork to the west edge of Brock Meadow where a comparatively easy course would bring it to an intended curve in the north west corner. When Keef delivered the next load of rail he said he would include a quantity of second hand material in good condition but of Continental section. He did. So we kept this separately until we came to a spot where there was a straight run and we could lay it altogether; the rail has a taller web so to make joints with the British standard section demands a compound fishplate, one that requires more time to produce. Meanwhile, one of the hobby boys who lived locally showed his father the unhelpful mound of ground through which the Railway's next phase of The Deviation must pass. In no time a mechanical digger plus driver had arrived and within the day had dug a most acceptable cutting through the offending obstruction. A bottle of (Scotch) Whisky was a pleasant form of thanks, which had saved us quite six months of manual digging. Certain boys were given an

unexpected lesson in driving the machine while others looked on enviously and wished that their hobby involved such opportunities.

In Autumn 1977, the two carriages comprising 'The Company Offices' were in the last stages of decay; but they had been a bargain-buy at £5 each, delivered. We planned to burn them or allow the Malvern Fire Brigade the pleasure! I had second thoughts. The Dean bogie van was the worst but I knew that a similar vehicle was preserved on the Severn Valley Railway at Bridgnorth. I also knew that a neighbour, Michael Fitzer, wanted a 'Pig's Boudoir' on his local farm so we decided to cut the body in half. The swine could well and truly enjoy Great Western hospitality!

The second body was a different proposition. Its origins were still a mystery. We knew it had been owned by one of the South Wales railway companies, that it was in the category of a guard's passenger luggage brake van, had been carried on six wheels and passed to the Great Western Railway in 1923. We had searched all the usual places for identification without success. Then one day I had a phone call from the Chairman of

Opposite: *The Railway said farewell to the smaller of the two 'Company Offices' in June 1978 when it was craned onto a road low-loader, destined for the Industrial & Maritime Museum in Cardiff.*

J.I.C. Boyd

Early in 1986 we completed the first of three ballast wagons, seen here standing on the recently-finished turntable. The wagons had springless but equalised bogies to a design based on Hornby products of the 1920s. Steel, timber and wheel castings were donated; outside body frames were of steel; the end drop doors slid in lengths of main-line point rodding.

J.I.C. Boyd

Priming severely, 'BROCK' bursts out from the tunnel in April 1976 and showers passengers with boiling water. The drain clearing is still in process and new cutting walls are going up.

J.I.C. Boyd

the Strathspey Railway at Boat of Garten. He was restoring a Highland Railway van in the stables of his Malvern home and needed some brass furniture for the doors. Could we help? We could. There was a box of surplus brass hinges off the carriage and as I packed them I noticed the lettering '*RR*' on the backs of each. So, the School possessed a Rhymney Railway vehicle body built by The Gloucester Railway Carriage & Wagon Co. Ltd. about 1900. It was certainly the last to survive. Without delay I telephoned a friend who was the Curator of the Industrial & Maritime Museum in Cardiff. '*Could he give some tender loving care, and a new home, to this historic vehicle?*', I asked. '*It needs restoration and mounting on a suitable chassis*'. To the incredulity of the School, a colossal mobile crane accompanied by a lorry arrived from Cardiff. The carriage body was lifted in a giant sling onto the lorry and, in no time, the pair disappeared down the road again, bringing down telephone wires as it did so. With the removal of both the carriage bodies, the DLR lost covered accommodation and for a time we had to be satisfied with the workshop behind the School. The appearance of 'HOYLAND DOWN' station was utterly changed. It was now spacious, light and airy. At the same time, though we had lost a carriage the nation had gained a historic vehicle. I think GH would have approved.

Coinciding at this time was the demise of my School Manager post and the appointment of a new Headmaster who was of the time-honoured calibre of being of the Latin-and-Cricket persuasion with little time for any occupation which made the hands dirty.

The little-by-little advance of the Railway (too tedious to detail) as it joined up with the original formation again and formed a loop by so doing, left us with an intriguing half-inch (12.7mm) gap in the track between the new and the old. With a small ceremony, we cut a suitable length of rail and closed the gap; it is still identifiable today. Due to subsequent relaying with better quality material, we enjoyed a second similar ceremony in the snow some years later.

Another of those lucky contacts had paved the way to this end. A considerable embankment was needed to take the line round the south edge of the Duck Pond and we were faced with the now-familiar thoughts of the several years ahead which would be needed to accomplish this. One day, a lady on the staff told us her husband's building firm was moving from Cheltenham and their Yard had to be cleared. Would we like its contents?

'*Delighted*', I said. So almost the whole embankment was built up in new bricks. The firm was clearly a major contractor for the building of Public Toilets, as the bricks were mostly white and reflected their intended use!

At this period I was visited by an old friend who had a 2ft. gauge railway in his vicarage garden, the never-to-be-forgotten Rev. Teddy Boston. He and his wife had brought along another couple, Norman Livingstone and his wife to see The Downs Light Railway. Norman was a talented engineer recently retired from a West Midlands car manufacturer and owned a $7^1/_4$ ins. gauge railway in the considerable grounds beside his house. The DLR gave them all great pleasure. Affairs on the DLR had reached a difficult stage (haven't I said this before?) where we were trying to service somewhat monumental civil engineering work then underway, with the life-expired bogie wagons which had served since about 1930. Anticipating troubles to come, we had already embarked on their replacement and built the body for the first of three we required, intending to use the rather unsuitable bogies off the old vehicles. Norman, clearly impressed by the boys' efforts generously offered to make free of charge six new bogies compatible with the new wagon bodies. The bogies are still in use and have run many miles.

The junction where the new railway re-joined itself to the old route beside the Ballast Platform required a new turnout. Having previously achieved what might have seemed to be impossible with steel fabrications, the construction of a complete turnout for this junction appeared not too difficult. The major snag was that being 20 ft. long it was far too long for our workshop. However, there was an unused building (which eventually came to an unhappy ending in 1984) which I judged to be suitable and, by devious enquiry, we were permitted to transfer our workshop, the carrot being that we would create a more suitable venue for the School's maintenance staff. It was, and still is.

When the time for our removal drew nigh, we had an impressive fall of snow. To have carried our benches and all the other impedimenta down hill to our new home, would have taxed the energies of even the enthusiastic but, by turning the benches upside down and loading them with our belongings, we were able to glissade over the frozen snow to the doors of the venue. One bench got away on the ice and partly demolished an entrance door! We christened the place with a plate on the door, 'WHITWORTH', after Joseph Whitworth the famous

If you like sloshing about in water and mud, this is the place for you. The east end of the tunnel, being perpetually flooded, had the track lifted in February 1976 to check for blocked field drains. This was only partially successful as the cause of the trouble was found elsewhere.

J.I.C. Boyd

Opposite: *It is the 7th June 1978 and the Railway is open for the Colwall Village Fête. Braithwaite is now the senior driver who has just released a sticking safety valve on 'GEORGE'.*

J.I.C. Boyd

mechanical engineer. We hoped that the Headmaster would ask us for the origin of the title but he was much too cunning to fall for our ploy.

Soon we had all the bits of the new turnout cut and laid out on 'WHITWORTH's floor. It was a wonderful introduction to sawing rails, cutting steel plate and working out the measurements full-size in chalk on the floor. We had to cut all rails by hand as electric drills were over-stretched and soon expired. Today we have no such problems - everything is done by machine. The 'launch' through the doors of 'WHITWORTH' was almost ten months after the 'laying down of the keel'. It had been an excellent example of the School motto '*Aedificandum Est*' (It is being built).

'BROCK', the new locomotive, had not fared well since delivery in 1975. This was made worse by the high expectations which we all held; it was to be the 'Secret Weapon' in the DLR armoury. Compared with any engine that had gone before, it epitomised our 'Big Engine' policy and in the eyes of the boys anything which was big was bound to be powerful and without fault. It took some weeks to assess the troubles; a shower of boiling water from out of the chimney and down the driver's neck due to priming, seemed to be incurable. The exhaust beat was lumpy and suggested the valve timing was adrift; the injector was moody. The boys were mystified and I was apprehensive.

We fitted a type of sieve in the steam dome to deter the hot water from entering into the delivery pipe. It made a slight improvement. Inspection and measurement followed and we feared the firebox crown was too high and the steam space too small; the engine was trying to run on hot water rather than steam! The irregular exhaust could not be cured by any setting of the valves and much, much later we identified this and related problems. The home-made injector was replaced by a commercial 'Buffalo' pattern which was expensive but reliable. We all learned much from these defects.

When running, the valve gear of 'BROCK' made a distinctive knock, and as a knowledgeable visitor exclaimed as a train approached, '*Knock, knock, here comes Brock*'. Worse, the '*Improved Hackworth*' valve gear as then fitted, had a playful habit of disintegrating in the New Road Tunnel, or equally testing, in the long grass of Brock Meadow where recovery of components was accompanied by wasps, hay fever and creepy-crawlies. The dismembered parts had often to have surgery and on several occasions disappointed passengers had to be sent away, their expectations unfulfilled. It would be 1997 before a benefactor allowed 'BROCK' to undergo severe remedial treatment at the Works of Alan Keef Ltd.

Despite the technical imperfections of 'BROCK' which, had they affected an internal combustion engine similarly, it would

have been put it out to grass, the engine kept going in the manner of all steam locomotives. What is more the boys loved it! Two boys could sit side by side on the tender and instruction by example became the norm. Every now and again girls would join the Hobby (but never alone); it gave us great pleasure to see two steam trains headed by 'BROCK' and 'TUBBY' whose drivers were sisters, operating the system alone with the minimum of supervision.

As with all railways, the affects of age were becoming apparent. The deep cutting at the eastern approach to the New Road Tunnel had been waterlogged for some years and hopefully we had tried to cure this by digging and laying new field drains. It was not until the large drain under the tunnel was discovered and cleared that trouble was largely overcome. However, the constant flooding had now undermined the cutting's retaining walls so we called in Alan Lloyd with his earth scraper to pare down and lessen the steepness of the sides. We rebuilt the cutting walls ourselves - no small job for the Hobby.

The Southport-built bogie wagons of 1930s origin which had been rebuilt more than once, went to the blacksmith for further alteration of the frames. On return we fitted new wooden seating but were careful not to take all the sharpness off its edges; a little discomfort reminds passengers that there may be others who want a ride!

Sometime afterwards, the Headmaster left for pastures new and I was surprised to receive a telephone call before the new Headmaster took office. His message went something like this: *'James, I have just bought you a Public Telephone Box for the Railway station platform'*. I was stunned and could only reply: *'Why? Do we need one?'* He assured me that all important stations had one and he was sure we would wish ours to thus demonstrate its superior status with this feature. I explained that everything on the DLR had to be of a utilitarian nature. *'For what purpose could we use it?'* I asked, and the reply came back, *'Well, it would LOOK nice'*. Thankfully, the Box went elsewhere but our initial conversation was not a good augury.

It was at this time that I outlined my battle with Authority over the years to a fellow Old Downian and School Governor. I explained that I felt the Governors did not perhaps fully understand the value of the educational assets we owned, in respect of the Railway and its Engineering bias. My listener confirmed my suspicions in that the Railway was held to be a plaything and the Board knew nothing of its educational

potentials. Together we hatched a plan to form a Charitable Trust to promote and support the Railway, admirably followed by *'to keep it out of the hands of well-meaning Headmasters and Governors'*. Our plan was vented at the next meeting of Governors but was not well received. They viewed it as a ploy to invite all our friends to come and play trains. By means of some clandestine canvassing we succeeded in persuading doubting Governors of our integrity and at their next meeting, the idea was accepted to a background of cautionary reservations. Thus came into being The Downs Light Railway Trust.

Returning to the Railway; now that 'BROCK' was, in comparison with 'GEORGE' and 'TUBBY', the engine that would be our first choice to use, we gave some serious thought to the motive power position. Although 'Sir' had kept his thoughts to himself, he was planning to put 'TUBBY' and 'GEORGE' out to grass and, subject to finance, to build a petrol-engined unit which would be used when urgent need was evident. To have breathed such plans for the two locomotives would be akin to heresy; they were the first engines which Old Downians asked to see when they made a return visit. Amongst the Trustees it was a different matter and in our biannual meeting I exchanged ideas about a petrol-engined locomotive, without mentioning the steam engines. The scheme was accepted with enthusiasm, but if any additional motive power was obtained, 'HOYLAND DOWN' engine shed could not hold it all.

For many years the Boys' Hall had been graced with a fine Chamber Organ which was used for evening services, played and pumped by boys 'on duty'. This instrument required drastic overhaul and it was decided to sell it. Its place in the Hall would be taken by 'GEORGE' and tender which today stands on a length of track at the west end of the Hall; some Trustees would like to witness it on DLR rails again!

Our intention was to prepare a design and drawings for an internal combustion-powered locomotive without delay, and seek out a suitable builder. But nature intervened. During a February night in 1984 we had a mini-hurricane which funnelled northwards up the New Road and flattened everything in its path. I was awoken by the bedside phone before it was light and a breathless voice asked me if the storm had kept us awake. It had not; it must have been very local. The voice said I ought to come up to School immediately as it was feared there had been considerable damage around the Railway. Once at School

Disparity in size and power is apparent as 'GEORGE' and 'BROCK' stand on The Deviation curve in July 1979. The curve was still in the process of being increased in height . . . . a very slow business.

J.I.C. Boyd

Following a visit to Milner Engineering at Chester for essential remedial work, the firm's proprietor (John Milner) has returned with a much-improved 'BROCK'. He is clearly enjoying the opportunity to verify the results on the DLR.

J.I.C. Boyd

The boys are not at all despondent when another 10 tons of Clee Hill ballast drops from the lorry onto the loading platform. The new wagons are beginning to look well-used.

J.I.C. Boyd

Left: *Any suitable material helps to build the formation. These were bricks intended to build a Public Convenience in Cheltenham, but they fell off a lorry near the DLR in March 1982!*   Below: *Delivery lorries become heavier and break up the back road to the School kitchens. In November 1983, a gang digs out the level crossing prior to renewal in concrete. And which humorist chalked up the warning sign?*

J.I.C. Boyd

Below: *In 1983 'TUBBY' was undergoing a transformation so as to make it more comparable in appearance with 'BROCK'. A tall, longer chimney looks promising, as does the new cab. A mock-up dome cover made from a jam tin and coated with clay shaped to profile, is being assessed for appearance.*

J.I.C. Boyd

and in the gloom of dawn one could see that where had been the ex-Cadbury building (now our workshop) there was nothing. The large shed beside 'HOYLAND DOWN' used for Estate storage wasn't there either, nor were the big willows which flanked the New Road. I had seen enough, turned back and went home to await daylight. The devastation was very local. Most of the main School had escaped but a large tree had flattened the Railway's workshop and its splintered timbers were sandwiched between the trunk and the ground. At this point a digression must intervene.

Compared with the large controls in 'BROCK's commodious cab, the boys found it difficult to find and operate the small

Here on the growing embankment at the southern end of The Deviation in March 1984 the stock of new rails from Workington came to an end. Beyond, the Railway faced the dual problem of finding tons of material to build up the embankment and of obtaining further rail. Perched on unstable ground, two boys with six jam tins combine to assemble a railway.

J.I.C. Boyd

brass fittings bunched together under the low cab roof on 'TUBBY' and suggested that something might be done. The simplest and cheapest scheme was to build a bigger cab, but this would give the chimney and dome a puny appearance in comparison. It was decided to proceed with a new cab and put a sleeve in the chimney to make it taller. A higher dome would have to be fabricated. To preserve the appearance of the whole we experimented with a series of mock-up cabs of various outlines, made from heavy-duty commercial cardboard cartons. We made our choice and cut the new cab from sheet metal, affixing half-round brass to the raw openings, and were well pleased with the result especially as the locomotive no longer looked so diminutive beside 'BROCK'. There were still a number of things to do at this stage, so we had taken the engine into 'WHITWORTH', putting it on the bench for the purpose. Then came the hurricane!

Approaching the debris of the shattered 'WHITWORTH' we were confident that the damage done to 'TUBBY' would be beyond repair so imagine our shock at seeing it, largely untouched, standing on the bench in a cocoon of space surrounded by tiles, beams and so on. However, the engine had survived being hit by the falling roof because a main supporting truss was being held up by the engine's new chimney! 'TUBBY' was to run again but our workshop was beyond repair so, until a replacement could be found, certain jobs were put on 'Hold'.

The Headmaster understood the Railway's dire need for premises and, having a full quota of problems himself, instructed me to '*get on with it*'. I set off for Gloucester to see the School's insurers and obtained the rough figure we might expect in respect of the workshop and our Claim for damages. I prepared drawings for a wooden building adequate to house a moderate number of children on the hobby, which, with sudden inspiration, I conjectured could stand where the former 'Company Offices' had been and, with cantilevered roof overhang, could double up as a station building providing some weather protection. I set off on a tour to find a builder used to agricultural construction and I was lucky to trace a farm nearby with suitable experience. Facts and figures were given to the Headmaster, but three weeks later a Board Meeting decided the Governors would take over the matter themselves, employ an architect, with whom I was ordered to liase, and find a builder. The appointed architect was to receive his statutory fee as a percentage of the cost. As the Board's chosen builder for the architect's design was up-market of my choice, the cost of the building plus the architect's fee was several thousand pounds above budget. The Railway Trustees were far from pleased when they learned that they would be expected to fund a considerable portion of the additional amount.

The architect was no more to be seen but in August 1984 the builders arrived; the School was on holiday and, being concerned that all was well with the workshop construction, I surprised the workmen who were just setting out the dwarf walls. The whole area was covered by a thick carpet of stone, stolen from the Railway's ballast platform. I insisted on seeing, for the first time, a copy of the architect's drawing. The men were laying out the foundations to the effect that no track could be run into the building to facilitate rolling stock repairs. One face of it did not give a safe clearance from the running line and worst of all the height of the floor was such that the window bottoms came too high in the walls to throw light into the building at a suitable height for the children. Appalled at this lack of communication, I went home and gave vent to the architect's office!

The new workshop should have become a showpiece and an example of the School's forward thinking; it was neither. The Trustees paid the share of costs with ill grace and left it to 'Sir' to the make the best of a bad job. At least we took comfort in the improved heating of the new premises. The original site of 'WHITWORTH' was grassed-over and landscaped.

The Railway Workshop was crushed during a mini-hurricane in February 1984 while 'TUBBY' was standing on a bench inside. The roof was partly held up by the engine's chimney.

J.I.C. Boyd

Replacement of the storm-wrecked Workshop came in the form of this architect-designed building erected by contractors during the School holidays. It is sited wrongly; the windows are undersized and too high above bench level. The DLR was powerless to interfere but addressed some of the defects later. September 1984.

J.I.C. Boyd

Chapter 9
Through Thick and Thin
1985 - 1990

Many times 'Sir' had been asked if the Railway was open to the public but his answer was always a firm '*No*'. He would add, with truth, that this was a classroom and not an Amusement Park, or that our insurance did not cover outsiders. But 'Sir' could be manipulated and we did begin to have visits from Special and Blind Schools, Church Choirs, Scouts, Guides and the like. On these occasions we would run two trains, having one loading at 'HOYLAND DOWN' whilst the other made its journey round the line; when the latter returned it would stop in the passing loop whilst the other train, now loaded, left the platform. The train detained in the loop could then run forward into the station and unload. Passing trains had their dangers; a large dog, in charge of a small girl, escaped off the platform and ran down the line chased by its keeper. Both dog and girl were trapped between a stationary and outgoing train; the girl was spun round but kept her feet, and the dog escaped. 'Sir' nearly had a fit but all ended well! In consequence no dogs are now admitted, and the distance between the tracks at the loop has been increased.

Although 'TUBBY' was easier to drive and its appearance was slightly enhanced, as an engine to haul trains 'Sir' was quite sure it was not as effective as in the early 1930s when it had six coupled driving wheels. When the regulator was opened to start a train, the engine would rear up like a circus horse, with its driving wheels spinning hopelessly. The total wheelbase was 52 inches but the four driving wheels occupied a wheelbase of only 13 inches . . . . in fact, the distance between the flanges of the driving wheels on each side was so minimal it was impossible to pass a finger between them. This was causing the engine to rock like a seesaw from end to end so that it spent little time with all four driving wheels firmly on the track. The fault had been instigated as a result of the last rebuilding in the 1930s.

The boiler seemed to be good enough to put new frames under it to accommodate a revised wheel arrangement. We agreed that something needed to be done, so out came the pencil and paper but it was a waste of time as the Trust had insufficient funds to do anything.

Constructive thought now turned to an old subject. Why not build a petrol-engined machine and put 'TUBBY' on one side until we could afford to deal with it? One of our Trustees with experience and a suitable workshop, offered to do the work. More detailed planning produced a six-wheel chassis (all wheels coupled and sharing the adhesive weight), robustly constructed to the fullest dimensions the New Road Tunnel would allow. The driver would sit at one end in a sideways position so as to have a clear view of the line in each direction. A two-stroke petrol engine coupled to a hydraulic unit via a flat industrial belt would drive it. There was a chain drive from here to the rear axle; the final drive was by rodding.

To save expense, completion would be done in our '*Fitting-Out Basin*', i.e. the workshop. We looked forward to delivery with anticipation; here would be a most useful tool both in service and for education. It arrived on a glorious summer day in 1986. Its debut that afternoon was marred for 'Sir' as he noted obviously feeble components more suited to model engineering and, at the same time, tried to stifle a bad dose of hay fever!

The builder, Derek Williams of Newport (an Old Downian), enjoyed the test runs hugely; with several bogie wagons on the rear it was splendidly powerful and clearly would form an excellent means for teaching young drivers. The controls were simple and School holidays then being upon us, 'Sir's five-year-old grandson soon mastered its principles and became the first accredited driver. With the coming of Autumn, we brought the

A new phase in locomotion marked the arrival of a petrol-hydraulic machine built by a Trustee and delivered in the Summer 1986. Seen here under test, it was below DLR specification and failed to stand up to our rigorous requirements . . . .

. . . . All our hopes had hung on the potential of the new locomotive with its instant availability and on which the boys' experience would be widened. Within weeks we spent much time on our knees sorting out its teething problems.

J.I.C. Boyd

chassis into the workshop and set about the bodywork. 'Sir's familiarity with the unfrequented parts of School quickly produced the components of the former laundry machine and redundant steel furniture from the office; it was all of sturdy sheet metal and proved excellent for our purpose. Everyone wanted to participate. It was intended to put a cab at one end as the boys wanted that 'being inside' sensation whilst driving; adults might have to endure a 'wrap around' position. We made a steel strip former the size and shape of the tunnel bore and began dummy runs with it held temporarily in place. Whilst the tunnel may be of consistent dimensions, the track inside the bore was not and was off-centre in places. Consequently we had to pare down the cab height accordingly.

An early experience when 'Sir's grandson was driving involved a derailment in the tunnel. The engine left the rails,

jammed itself in a derailed position and could not be lifted as the cab roof was almost hitting the tunnel roof. The small driver was able to escape by crawling out of the back onto a wagon behind. He telephoned home the same evening, beginning with, '*It was not my fault, but . . . .* '! The reason for the derailment was not obvious at the time but was the first of a number of faults, to our growing dismay. Importantly the wheels were too dainty by DLR standards and the horrific angularity sometimes adopted by the side rods showed the wheels were loose on their axles. Further unhelpful signs revealed themselves and 'Sir's initial reaction came true - whilst suited perhaps to 5 inch gauge, it was not robust enough for the rugged conditions of the DLR.

We had a good friend in Welwyn who would put matters right; he collected the offending chassis and we put our faith in his expertise. John Fleetwood Shawe of Welwyn rebuilt the chassis to more robust standards, with heavier wheel sets and coupling rods plus a 2-stroke Villiers engine. The boys had insufficient strength to successfully achieve lanyard starting and this was a disadvantage that limited the unit's potential; however he did not disappoint. On the engine's return a quick inspection showed we had chosen wisely; the engine was above our specification and on test was everything we needed. The body was re-assembled, painted all but the ends in Lizard Green and the ends in bright Yellow. Wheels and motion were bright Red and brass nameplates 'TIM' were affixed to recognise the Trustee, Tim Cadbury, who had funded the construction. The whole event caused the numbers on the Hobby to surge to the extent that we had to limit them drastically.

During May 1986 the workshop was given an official opening by a Member of the European Parliament, Sir James Scott-Hopkins. He reminded his listeners how industry was desperately short of Engineers, especially in our adjacent West Midlands. He congratulated the School for its vision as epitomised by our workshop.

The School had accepted girls since the late 1970s but for some years none had joined the Railway Hobby. When the hobby boys heard a rumour that a girl was joining them, they were dismayed. It took courage for a lone girl to do this. 'Sir' was delighted by this development but his enthusiasm was dented when a group of four girls joined! Anxious to encourage others and finding that the four were promising, they were given instruction on 'GEORGE', and took tests of proficiency within the confines of 'HOYLAND DOWN'. Sharing the experience of driving, point control and supervision between them, they made a careless mistake and 'GEORGE' left the rails to be thrown on its side. The driver, sitting on the tender (which was unaffected), leapt off; she and the three others took to their heels up the meadow towards Brock Wood. 'Sir' was left with the boys to clear up the accident. Never having such experience before and being left speechless, they could only laugh! We learned never to take girls in a group; individuals have since proved most rewarding.

'Sir' is fanatical about Irish railways so when he was offered a signal off the Great Southern Railways in Dublin he made arrangements to collect it on a forthcoming visit. He convinced himself that this was just the thing needed by the DLR for controlling trains in and out of 'HOYLAND DOWN'. It took six

An opportunity to collect sufficient materials to build an ex-main line semaphore signal, albeit from Dublin, was too good to miss although it required two journeys there to bring all the parts over. We erected the post with the help of the School's scaffolding. The signal controls incoming trains arriving at 'HOYLAND DOWN' . . . . it is not an ornament.

J.I.C. Boyd

months to erect and further time to build a suitable operating lever in the station. The importance of other schemes then took priority; though the signal could be operated the lever was never connected and the hollow soft-wood 'post' which had been made for it was showing signs of rot. Subsequently the signal had to be dismantled and is being replaced with an oak post.

With 'BROCK' being the first example of our Big Engine policy, we turned our minds towards 'TUBBY'. Had the engine any potential for a rebuild, especially conversion from a four coupled wheel arrangement to six coupled where it might overcome its lack of adhesion? We made a full-size drawing of the existing frames showing the position of the axles in relation to the cylinders; because we intended to re-use the existing valve gear, we were obliged to retain some of the axle centres. Another generous Trustee took the engine in hand and stripped it down to the frames. 'Sir' visited his workshop at this stage and was astonished to see 'TUBBY', for the first time, in its 'naked' condition. Readers will remember that the engine had started life as 'STANTOR' and had endured several rebuilds. Close scrutiny at this naked stage revealed that its condition was still unchanged since its days as 'STANTOR'. This would mean that the rebuild on which we now intended to embark would be wasted as the thin weak frames and cross-stretchers would never carry the substantial changes we had in mind. As 'Sir' lay in bed he grappled with several outrageous ideas, usually ending up with some ridiculous name for a new creation and having to begin his thoughts all over again! One thing was certain, it would be a waste of time to assemble 'TUBBY' again and after we had

cannibalised it for useful parts, what survived could be sold. In the event, this is what happened.

We began to look for advice, a builder and something the Trust could afford (we seem to have been at this stage before!). Our friend at Welwyn was too busy so we turned to another good friend, John Milner of Milner Engineering Chester Ltd. of Chester who, apart from being contractors to the aerospace industry had also been building steam locomotives since 1972. John proved to be as excited about the project as ourselves. To satisfy the sentimentalists, we intended to incorporate as many parts of 'TUBBY' as it was feasible to use but most were too worn or otherwise unsuitable. In the ultimate, the bulk of the engine would be new. We referred to this new creation as 'TUBBY II'.

The success of the 2-6-2 wheel arrangement, together with the general dimensions of 'STANTOR's first rebuilding by Morse, pointed the way. A new boiler, surplus to requirements, was offered at a reasonable price by another company. It was not easy to accommodate an available boiler with a chosen wheel arrangement, and the dimensions of the motion and driving wheels; furthermore the length of engine and tender was restricted by space in the engine shed and length of the turntable. In the event, extension rails gave further availability to the

Fourteen years after commencing The Deviation, the track was nearing the point where it rejoined the old line to form a return loop. Another embankment was needed around the Boating Pond. The inevitable ballasting gang can almost anticipate 'finis'.

J.I.C. Boyd

Standing on the final but incomplete embankment of The Deviation in February 1986, the first train poses to mark the occasion. The line beyond the train is as yet unconnected. 'TUBBY' looks quite convincing in its new guise but the track requires much levelling.

J.I.C. Boyd

Below: *'BROCK' is approaching Brock Hill Junction in 1987 where the green single line token will be exchanged with the pointsman.*

The Downs School

An urgently-needed feature was a high-level ramp to the roadside for transfer to and from road vehicles; under construction here, it all looks a little flimsy. It has become, in effect, an essential train-stabling head-shunt when three engines/two trains operate simultaneously. Dec. 1991.

J.I.C. Boyd

Trackwork is not kind to the knees. Here old sleepers are being replaced in situ with new. Working with ratchet-fitted spanners and a detachable socket to fit the nut, the boys soon achieve the required skills. 1987.

J.I.C. Boyd

*A **double-headed train** enters 'HOYLAND DOWN' during the 1987 Commemoration celebrations.*

J.I.C. Boyd

turntable, these being cantilevered off each end and the locking system modified to suit. Having virtually completed the locomotive, John decided that he could not let it leave his Works with the original tender, which now looked somewhat tired and out of place. His son, Stephen, volunteered and built a completely new tender body to suit although the original bogies were retained.

'TUBBY II' (now in fact 'JAMES BOYD') owes much to overseas narrow gauge practice, especially of the Indian metre gauge. 'BROCK' on the other hand, favours a sugar plantation prototype. The former requires more expertise from the boys, and gives a superb ride. As in other issues, each boy has his favourite engine and the DLR comes into its own when 'JAMES BOYD', 'BROCK' and 'TIM' are 'let out' for the day.

Whilst the Trust was kept informed as to progress and occasionally 'Sir' found it convenient to drop in to see developments at Chester, we kept fairly quiet as to what was afoot. John had generously offered to build the locomotive by charging us only for the materials but nothing for the labour. Indeed the saga of the DLR is punctuated with copious benefactors. Construction was to be fitted in between the firm's commercial orders and so a speedy delivery was not even contemplated; in the event manufacture continued through 1990 and 1991 and was the last commercial steam locomotive to be built by Milner Engineering Chester Ltd.

Now we needed a place on the Railway where the current use of trailers or small lorries could be accommodated. At the time, the Railway terminated (or began) in the wartime turntable pit site across the lane from 'HOYLAND DOWN' station. There was still a concrete wall round most of the pit. The level crossing over the lane also required rebuilding from its wartime height, because the Headmaster had been talked into buying a load of 'Motorway Surplus' tarmac from a loquacious Irishman onto whose lorry it had gratuitously fallen! The said gentleman had then tipped and spread his load so that the Railway was deep beneath several inches of material suitable to carry six-axle lorries. There was no alternative but to extend the line southward from 'HOYLAND DOWN', cut through the 'Motorway' and demolish such portions of concrete walling as lay on our route. Beyond this it would be necessary to dig a cutting, remove some young trees and build a considerable embankment to reach the roadside, climbing as it was extended to reach a suitable height. Lorries etc. could then back up to the end of track and transfer their load by means of a short, portable bridging piece. The amount of earth required to build up the embankment took up all the adjacent cutting spoil, and more. When not in use this head-shunt, as it became, is invaluable for storing a second train out of the way when we operate the three-engines and two-trains system on busy days. When stock transfer is not anticipated there is a 'portable' buffer stop in place.

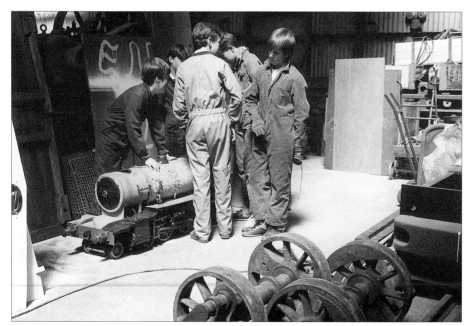

A visit in July 1989 to Alan Keef Ltd. enables the boys to experience an engineering works where a variety of railway equipment is made. The small engine at their feet is the DLR's 'TUBBY'.

J.I.C. Boyd

Chapter 10
Into the New Millennnium
1991 - 2000

A perpetual problem for most railways is created by the existence of natural growth and the DLR is no exception. After the Second War there appeared several varieties of weedkiller: a specific agricultural type in liquid form was preferred and, having parents with farms or chemical stores, we had a supply of 'the needful' free of charge. A rather sophisticated sprayer was bought and was mounted, as required, on a wagon together with a galvanised water tank, as it was too far to return to 'HOYLAND DOWN' simply to refill the sprayer. Later on we built a four-wheeled wagon to carry the sprayer permanently which was fitted with a 6ft. sprayer bar at the front thus enabling us to spray the track and environs simultaneously. All this time the strength of weedkillers was increasing and the brand we used was taken off the market for all but commercial purposes. Today, weedkilling is done by the Estate staff at the beginning of May each year when the track is already disappearing and their assistance becomes vital. The spraying wagon was out of use until an indoor winter programme re-evaluated it for use as a passenger vehicle. A substantial movable box-shaped body is carried on a flat floor, which also serves to carry the guard during passenger working. The transformation is greatly successful and the best runner among our wagons.

A telephone call jerked 'Sir' into action; the new locomotive would arrive from Chester shortly, brought by John Milner and his son Stephen from Milner Engineering. We checked our roadside extension again, removed its temporary buffer stop and waited. Next day the trailer carrying both engine and tender arrived and backed up. John's meticulous fastenings were undone and, with the 'bridging piece' in place, the engine and tender were on DLR tracks within minutes. Before the afternoon was over, steam had been raised and the engine was running the circuit round Brock Meadow; considering it had only had a stationary test in the Chester workshop, everything went well. Only one thing was amiss, being the provision of a tender handbrake, which was added in due course.

Metallurgists tell us that it is unwise to quickly heat up dissimilar metals together as they expand at different rates. 'The Elephant's Trunk' fan installation did precisely that; it only took 20 minutes to raise steam. It was popular; it gave more time for running the engine. Determined to abandon the practice, 'Sir' had all the engines fitted with a connection into the blower pipe to allow a portable air compressor to be connected, the only drawback being that the DLR did not have a compressor at that time. This shortcoming was made good by the Church. Ledbury Parish Church, with which 'Sir' has close connections, made a request to use the School, its grounds and facilities on an August Sunday. It was arranged that the DLR be operational; the event was such a success that it was repeated the following year. As the School had made no charge, the Rector asked if anything was wanted for the DLR which the Church could donate. That was how St. Michael's compressor found its way to the Railway. The whole operation of steam raising is now much cleaner, safer and more efficient.

This development turned our thoughts to other features of the Railway that could be improved. For instance, 'TIM's engine as mentioned, with its lanyard pull-starting method (similar to a lawn mower) could only be started by someone strong enough to do it. Again, a generous Trustee came to our rescue; a replacement new 4-stroke 'Robin' Japanese engine with electrical start was fitted in 1995 by Alan Keef Ltd. of Ross-on-Wye, and at the same time 'TIM' was given a powerful horn and a headlight at each end. Thus equipped, a small but capable boy could do everything without assistance. The somewhat makeshift platform at 'HOYLAND DOWN' was something of an eyesore and an

The 'Big Engine' . . . .

The new, un-named 'Prairie-type' locomotive is tested by John Milner of the builders Milner Engineering Chester Ltd., after delivery in April 1992. The design is akin to Indian metre gauge practice and the engine incorporates parts of its predecessor, 'TUBBY'.

J.I.C. Boyd

A prestigious naming ceremony for the new locomotive was held in November 1992. Accompanied by a specially-composed fanfare from the brass of the School's Music Department, well-known Old Downian Philip Trevor-Jones unveiled the new nameplates 'JAMES BOYD'. Left to right: the Author, Philip Trevor-Jones, Andrew Auster (Headmaster) and Tim Cadbury (Trustee).

John Milner

Above: *The Engineers, with Hugh Nicklin, proudly display the new locomotive, as yet unnamed, now available along with 'BROCK' to cope with the DLR's requirements. To drive, each engine needs different skills of handling.*

A. Auster

Prior to the formal ceremonies , 'Sir' takes the controls of the 'Big Engine' for the first time. 'What on earth are all these knobs and gadgets for?'

John Milner

Raising steam. Patrick Keef passes on a few practical hints, including that of how to strike a match!

J.I.C. Boyd

outside contractor both lengthened and faced it with bricks. To separate the station from the Estate Shed behind, a long picket fence was built at the platform rear; this also has the merit of further safety. The Trustees provided the funding. The Estate staff re-laid the adjacent road crossing in concrete after the Hobby had rebuilt the track; this became imperative as heavier lorries delivering to the School became more frequent.

The Trustees held a prestigious naming ceremony in November 1992 to bestow the name 'JAMES BOYD' on the new engine. A well-known Old Downian, Philip Trevor-Jones, unveiled it by deftly pulling aside a suitably filthy and oily rag that hid the nameplates, accompanied by a specially-composed fanfare from the brass of the School's Music Department. 'Sir' had already put the manufacture of the nameplates in hand when the news was 'leaked' to him that they would not be wanted, and that ones carrying his own name had already been made at

Milner Engineering with the blessing of the other Trustees. 'Sir' was not altogether best pleased, feeling that 'TUBBY II' retained a tradition which went back to the first days of the DLR. But it was too late.

As to 'GEORGE', it has required much time and expense over the years. Being designed for garden railway use its small cylinders and large driving wheels are quite unequal to the rugged conditions of the DLR. The boiler steamed magnificently and it ran like a greyhound when not overloaded. However, with the arrival of the new engine, the time came when its length (9 ft. 8 ins.) in the engine shed had to be used for more suitable motive power and it was decided to 'retire' it.

Eventually, the Trustees decided to put 'BROCK' into first-class order so that its reliability could not be questioned. Now that John Milner had retired from the engineering business Messrs. Alan Keef Ltd. were chosen for the work. When the

It isn't often that we are asked to stop for a picture on a hot afternoon.

P.M. Keef

The Superintendent of the Line Andrew Thompson (who went on to read Engineering at Oxford), drives 'TIM' over Brock Hill Junction on a Families' Open Day in 1991.

Collection : The Downs School

'If I don't duck, will my head come off?' The New Road Tunnel looms.

Hugh Nicklin

The most recent steel-framed wagon discards features that have proved undesirable and embodies ideas gleaned from a railway on the Isle of Mull.

J.I.C. Boyd

Below: *The Head pays a visit to the boys who are prefabricating the track for the new ramp; on these welcome visits they are eager to explain their achievements. June 1998.*

J.I.C. Boyd

In the workshop, Tim Pennock struggles bravely to re-assemble the left-hand side rod on 'BROCK'. Spring 1997.

J.I.C. Boyd

Mrs. Griggs (Head Teacher) enjoys a lesson from Simon, our youngest driver. She found driving through the tunnel, 'exhilarating'. June 1998.

J.I.C. Boyd

Early morning at 'HOYLAND DOWN' shed sees steam raising taking place. The fire in 'BROCK' (foreground) is burning well, assisted by the compressor; the tender is being filled. 'JAMES BOYD's driver nonchalantly checks the coffee level in his flask before moving off. 'TIM' (distance) has already shunted the stock and stands at the platform.

J.I.C. Boyd

engine returned from them, a brief glance showed little evidence of change, the main improvement being the new outside motion and the wheel balance weights. If there was any doubt, the performance of the engine now spoke for itself. No longer the *'Knock, knock here comes . . .'* The Hackworth-type valve motion was retained but rebuilt and the cylinder drains were moved to a position where they would not be wiped off by various lineside obstructions, such as were frequently found on this unfenced site passing in part, through playing fields. It was the ultimate relief to have three reliable locomotives on hand; no more the lottery as to whether an engine would perform on an Open Day or whether its appearance would be cut short by some mischance; no chance to call on a substitute in those days. 'Sir's grey hairs bear witness.

'Sir' is often asked what opportunities exist for young people today who wish to continue their active participation with railways after they leave The Downs. *'How does Health & Safety affect the activity?' 'How different are those engaged on the Hobby today?' 'Could other Schools emulate?'* And so forth, are the usual questions raised. Between 1925 and 1951 there

was little opportunity for boys to be involved except under special circumstances. Former pupils, returning to their former haunts remark, *'Yes, I am enjoying my new school but it hasn't got a railway. I miss that most of all'.* Fortunately there are opportunities today which never existed before the l950s. The Talyllyn Railway was the first to offer participation through its Preservation Society and others followed. Young members of this Preservation Society do occasional training on the DLR; the Health & Safety Regulations recently introduced by the 'Nanny State' prevent such Societies from allowing their youngest members a genuine hands-on experience until they reach a certain age. The DLR on the contrary, expects its drivers to be proficient on non-steam working at the age of ten and on steam, a year later. The DLR is only as excellent as are the members of the Hobby. Its year-by-year efficiency varies with their ability and ambition.

There is no other similar railway forming part of the curriculum of any school in Great Britain. For longevity of existence it has no equal and it still fulfils the purpose for which it was created. 'Sir' is hopeful that it will survive indifference

It was a hot day. We gave some parents a ride behind 'TIM'. On re-entering 'HOYLAND DOWN' a stone jammed in the points derailed the wagon behind 'TIM', after which the whole train left the track. 'Sir' was greatly amused and assured the passengers that parents are not charged anything extra for this type of experience.

J.I.C. Boyd

Right: *1998. On selected days during the holidays, open days are arranged for members of the hobby when they create their own programme. This often involves two locomotives and two trains and develops their operating and driving skills to an extent not possible in term time.*

J.I.C. Boyd

'TIM' (left) has been fitted with a new engine, self-starter, headlamps and electric horn so becoming a most reliable, powerful and ever-ready locomotive. 'BROCK' (right) has Keef's replacement valve motion, new balance weights and backhead fittings. 1999.

J.I.C. Boyd

and endure whatever knife-edge crisis which may come its way. 'Sir' avers that the School taught him sufficient Latin to appreciate the translation of the School motto, *AEDIFICANDUM EST*. The DLR is the very epitome of that motto.

The Summer of 1998 was attended by some notable 'firsts'. A village event to raise money for charity witnessed an occasion on Brock Meadow the like of which had never been seen before. The meadow itself resembled a colourful funfair with a band in the centre. Three engines and two sets of passenger stock were in operation non-stop for $4^1/_2$ hours. The drivers' ages ranged from only 9 to 11 . . . . there were no derailments and no panic. The Trustees who attended, simply to supervise, were largely redundant so spent their time usefully by marshalling crowds on the platform and the queue up the road who were waiting for a train.

The Hobby has its ups and downs; only our youngest boys remained for the New Millennium to carry on the tradition and some newcomers were attracted to alternative hobbies where much less was demanded of them. Those who have looked on from a distance now see the fun we have in learning, and have decided to 'have a go'. It has always been thus, and long may it continue. Seventy-five years is quite an age for any miniature railway to have reached and again Geoffrey Hoyland would have undoubtedly been pleased!

We may reflect on the broader aspect of the DLR as part of the community. Colwall village was to mark the New Millennium with a Fun Day for the whole of the neighbourhood. The organisers, Colwall Rotary Club, asked for the Railway to be the centre of attraction, situated as it is around the perimeter of the Cricket Field on which the event would take place. We chose our customary method of using 'TIM', 'BROCK' and 'JAMES BOYD', two of which would be hauling a passenger train while the third rested (with its driver) on 'WINDERMERE' engine shed. We had four drivers among the boys. Two supervising adults were available to drive when the boys became exhausted. We lit up at 11 am., test ran the trains and started a service at 2 pm. We tried to run the last train at 6 pm but the queue for the train demanded that we continue; at 7 pm the boys were ready to collapse. We had carried over 400 persons and had to disappoint others for whom time had run out.

The event raised a considerable amount for charity and the whole Railway was run by the boys with minimum supervision and no mishaps. We made many good friends beyond the School and when exhausted but homeward bound, could reflect on how far things had come in seventy five years and how our persistence in supporting the DLR, when things looked hopeless, had been justified.

School Centenary Day.

The Headmaster, Chris Black (a non-qualified driver), has been persuaded to sit on 'BROCK' but will not be parted from his borrowed steaming hat or his piece of birthday cake! July 2000.

Anna Bennion

Photographed in June 2001, the Railway is very different from that witnessed by the author seventy years ago. Here, 'JAMES BOYD', designed and built by Milner Engineering Chester Ltd. in 1992, heads out around the meadow with a load of obviously delighted passengers. Richard Kempa is the driver and in the foreground are two of the Engineers; Simon Goldrick and Robbie Pringle. On the train in order from the front are Joe Dawson; Emily Hill; Rosalind Arscott; Mr. H.D.J. Nicklin; Elliot Hamer; Jessica Wilson; Mr. James I.C. Boyd and Joshua Williams.

Alistair Kerr Photography

Appendix 1
Personalities

FRANCIS (FRANK) FRAZER HOYLAND

Born in 1863, he was an uncle to Geoffrey Hoyland, the second Headmaster and later owner of The Downs School. He was an accomplished engineer and draughtsman, and owned a considerable collection of steam engines both stationary and locomotives, some being of his own building. He lived in Letchworth. Uncle Frank as he was known, became the rock on which the DLR was founded.

GEOFFREY HOYLAND (GH herein)

Born in 1889, Geoffrey Hoyland first came to The Downs in September 1911 as an Assistant Master but soon left for Cambridge to read History. He left Cambridge in 1915 to teach at the Lower School, Uppingham, eventually returning to The Downs in January 1919 as a Junior Partner. Shortly after his arrival he became engaged and married Dorothea Cadbury, daughter of George Cadbury. In January 1920 the couple took over the School.

In collusion with his Uncle Frank, he was the visionary who saw that boys had much to learn from activities apart from their conventional education. From participation in a railway, the boys learned leadership and teamwork; in them broader horizons and creative instincts were encouraged. His philosophy followed that of Edward Thring in that a school was primarily a society and not an institute for instruction; produce a good society and you have a good school. During his 20 years at The Downs he strived to fulfil his philosophy and in so doing greatly developed the School.

He was taken ill in the summer of 1940, was forced to retire and eventually died in June 1965. The Chairman of the Governors at that time paid tribute and wrote: '*Geoffrey Hoyland had created The Downs. He had breathed into it the breath of his own life. It remained part of him*'.

WILLIAM FRAZER HOYLAND

Frazer was stepbrother to Geoffrey Hoyland and a pupil at The Downs. He became a Junior Partner at the School in 1937 and Headmaster when GH retired in 1940. He saw the School safely through the difficult period of the War. Owing to wartime conditions and the problems brought thereafter, the DLR was largely inactive during his time. He carried forward the firm foundation established by Geoffrey Hoyland.

LILLIAN (CURLY) LAWRENCE

Lillian Lawrence was a well-known designer and builder of miniature steam locomotives and was a regular contributor to THE MODEL ENGINEER. He wrote under the pseudonym of 'L.B.S.C.' which was derived from 'London Brighton & South Coast Railway' on which he once worked. He was born in Paddington, London, in 1882 and married Mabel Hunt of Camberwell on the 2nd January 1908. He died on the 5th November 1967 having built 55 miniature steam locomotives during his lifetime and written thousands of articles on the subject.

R.H. MORSE

He was a former employee of the London Brighton & South Coast Railway and, in the 1920s, began building tools for model engineers and miniature locomotives (mainly to 9$\frac{1}{2}$ ins. gauge) at Elder Place, Brighton, before moving to Henfield. His first engine was 'RANMORE' and he was associated with several miniature railways at resorts and holiday camps. How his association with Geoffrey Hoyland began is not known, but it resulted in the first rebuilding of 'STANTOR'. He and his family visited The Downs School for about a week when the re-gauged 'TUBBY' and 'RANMORE' were delivered. His three small sons took great delight in playing with their father's bijou open wagons until there was a collision with opposing movements in the tunnel. A minor gallimaufry!

His work and name appeared frequently in THE MODEL ENGINEER. An unexpected link with the School was forged with installation of a vertical boiler and horizontal steam engine in 'the back railway carriage' in 1933. Again, the whole family returned to the School for the event. After Henfield, he also resided at South Woodham and Potter Heigham.

PARVER MODELS LTD.

This firm traded in model and miniature railways at 66a, Eastbourne Rd., Birkdale, Southport; in the decade before the Second War they offered a G.N.R. type 'Atlantic' locomotive in 2 ins. scale based on a Greenly design. The bogie wagons and bogies they supplied to the DLR are still in use.

WILLIAM M. SPRIGGS

He was resident at Acock's Green, Birmingham, 1908-1910 and was the father of Robert Spriggs who was a boy at The Downs until 1915 when, because of the Great War, the family emigrated to Quebec, Canada. He commissioned the building of

'STANTOR' and his notepaper in 1912 had a photograph on the heading showing the engine in his Birmingham garden. Spriggs and family visited England in 1922 and he met Greenly again; a letter to Greenly from Quebec in 1945 had the same letterhead featuring 'STANTOR'.

HENRY GREENLY

Henry Greenly was born on the 3rd June 1876 in Birkenhead on the Wirral. He became one of the leading figures at the turn of the century in the promotion of the hobby of model engineering and the building of small-scale garden railways and public railways, both in the UK and on the Continent.

He acted as design consultant for the Bassett-Lowke Company as well as several other well-known model engineering establishments of the day. Apart from writing what are now standard reference works on locomotive building he started his own magazine on the subject (*MODELS, RAILWAYS AND LOCOMOTIVES*) in 1908.

Whilst it is difficult to isolate oneself from his pioneering work in all areas of model engineering and miniature railways he is perhaps better known for the design and building of the 15 ins. gauge Romney, Hythe and Dymchurch Railway.

Appendix 2
Internal Combustion Locomotives

(No name) 4-wheeled Tractor
9½" gauge

1977	Built by Geoffrey Partridge.
c1980	Dismantled.

'TIM' 6-coupled Rail Tractor
9½" gauge

1986	New. Built by Derek Williams, Newport.
1989	Rebuilt 1989 by J.F. Shawe.
1995	New engine fitted with electric start by Alan Keef Ltd.

Appendix 3
Steam Locomotives

'STANTOR' 2-6-2 Tender Locomotive
7¼" gauge (later 9½" gauge)

1908 - 1910	Built for W.M. Spriggs.
1923	Arrived at The Downs per Frank Hoyland.
c.1928	Named 'TUBBY'.
1931 and 1933	Rebuilt and modified by R.H. Morse.
1937	Converted to 4-4-2 and 9½" gauge.
Cylinders (pre 1937)	2" dia. bore x 3¼" stroke.
Cylinders (post 1937)	2" dia. bore x 3" stroke.
Driving Wheels	7⅛" dia.

'MAUD' 2-6-0 Tender Locomotive
7¼" gauge
Great Western Railway outline

1919	Built by Neville Brindley Richards.
Pre 1929	Acquired by Geoffrey Hoyland for the DLR.
c1937	Sold.
Cylinders	1⅜" bore x 3" stroke.
Driving Wheels	7½" dia.

'RANMORE' 0-4-2 Tank Locomotive
9½" gauge   Scale: 2 in. = 1 ft.
London Brighton & South Coast Railway Class D

1930-31	Built by R.H. Morse, Brighton.
1937	Purchased by Geoffrey Hoyland for the DLR.
1942	Sold to Lawrence Redfern, Prestbury, Cheshire.
Early 1970s	Rebuilt by Coleby-Simkins Engineering.
Cylinders	2¼" dia. x 4½" stroke.
Driving Wheels	11" dia.

'GEORGE' 4-4-2 Tender Locomotive
9½" gauge   Scale: 2 in. = 1 ft.
Great Northern Railway outline

c.1939-40	Partially built by/for V.B. Burgoyne of Crowthorne, Berks. Completed by R.H. Morse to a Greenly/Bassett-Lowke design.
1941	Sold by Burgoyne per R.H.Morse to Geoffrey Hoyland.
1949-50	Repaired by Curwen & Newbury, Newbury.
1984-present	Out of use.
Cylinders	2⅜" dia. x 4" stroke.
Driving Wheels	13¼" dia.

'BROCK' 0-4-0T Tender Locomotive
9½" gauge
Freelance Narrow-Gauge

1971-74	Built by David Curwen, Devizes. Works No.4/71.
c1977	Boiler modified by Milner Engineering Chester Ltd.
1997	Partial re-build by Alan Keef Ltd.

'JAMES BOYD' 2-6-2 Tender Locomotive
9½" gauge
Freelance Narrow-Gauge

1992	Designed/built by Milner Engineering Chester Ltd. Utilised some parts from 'TUBBY' - mainly cylinders, valve gear and tender bogies. Fitted with new frames, wheelsets and rods plus a new boiler.

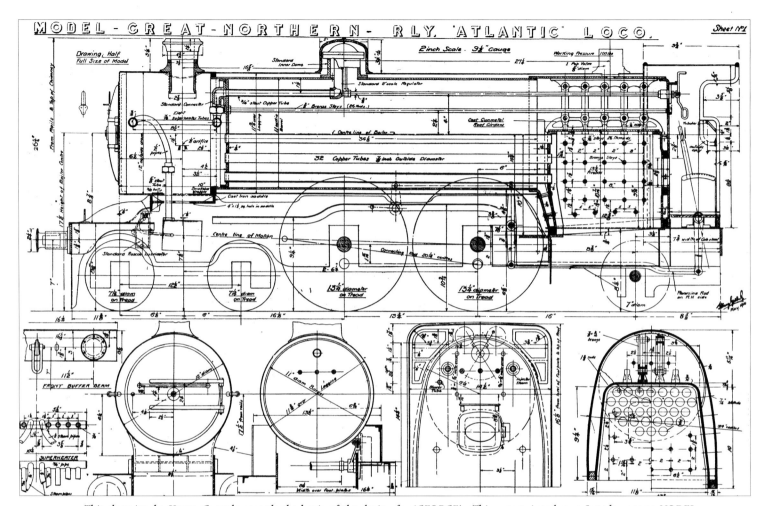

This drawing by Henry Greenly reveals the basis of the design for 'GEORGE'. This was printed as a Supplement to MODEL RAILWAYS AND LOCOMOTIVES in July 1910.

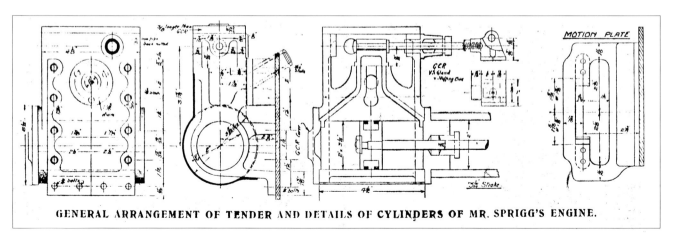

GENERAL ARRANGEMENT OF TENDER AND DETAILS OF CYLINDERS OF MR. SPRIGG'S ENGINE.

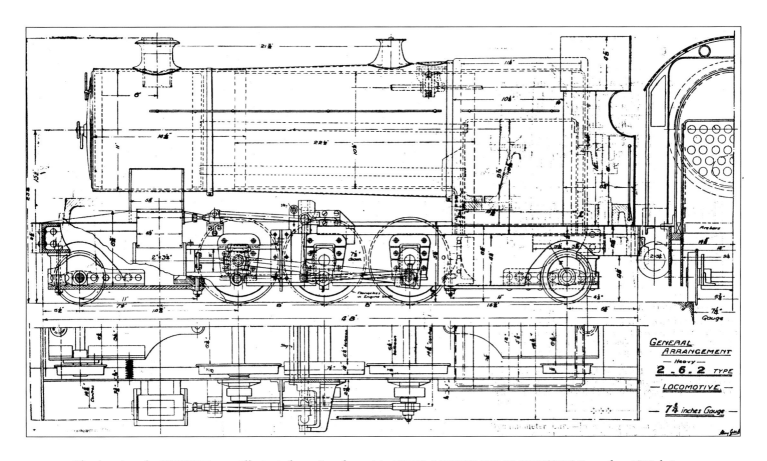

The drawings for 'STANTOR' were illustrated as a Supplement in MODEL RAILWAYS AND LOCOMOTIVES December, 1912, being described as 'Mr. W.M. Spriggs' model two inch scale narrow-gauge type locomotive'. The drawing is signed 'Henry Greenly'.
Opposite page bottom: The cylinder and motion plate drawing for 'STANTOR'.

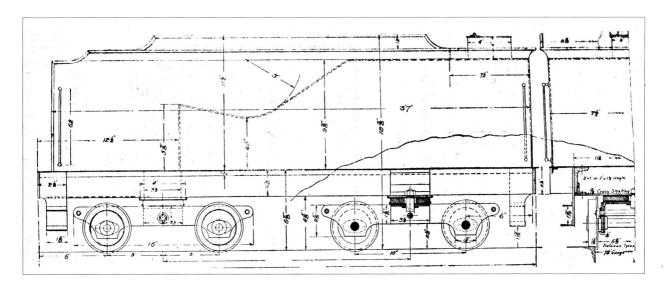

Appendix 4
Rolling Stock

Rolling Stock (7¼" gauge)

(1)	3 Open Bogie Wagons.	Built c1926. Diamond frame bogies, etc. by Bassett-Lowke Ltd. Timber plank construction, probably built locally. Not identical; one had an outside body frame. Not converted to 9½" gauge or numbered. Paint grey. Dismantled.
(2)	3 Open Bogie Wagons.	Supplied 1933 by R.H. Morse, Bramlands Lane, Woodmancote, Nr. Henfield. Identical; plate frame bogies. Converted to 9½" gauge 1937. Not numbered. Paint chocolate brown. Survived until 1976.
(3)	2 Flat Bogie Wagons.	Supplied 1933 by Parver Models Ltd., 66a, Eastbourne Rd., Birkdale. Cast frame bogies. Converted to 9½" gauge 1937. Lengthened 1971. Given high sides 1972. Rebuilt as well-wagons with longer frames and sit-astride bodies 1978 and numbered 2 & 3. Paint Lizard Green. In traffic.
(4)	1 Open Bogie Wagon.	Built by 1933. A single wagon with a shallow well in the floor. Originally fitted Parver type bogies but latterly had bogies off 'STANTOR's tender. Converted to 9½" gauge 1937. Paint chocolate brown. No number. Scrapped.

Rolling Stock (9½" gauge)

(5)	3 Open Bogie Wagons.	Built DLR 1976-80. Steel frames with DLR/Livingstone bogies. Two have sliding end doors; one has drop sides and ends. Nos. 4, 5, & 6. Bodies creosoted. In traffic.
(6)	Flat Bogie Wagon.	Built DLR 1993 (unfinished). Plate frame bogies. Steel frame. No. 7. Paint Lizard Green. (Convertible and designed for heavy duties).
(7)	Flat Wagon (4wh).	Built DLR 1994. Steel frame with removable box body (conversion from Weed Sprayer). Mainly used as guard's wagon on passenger trains. Paint grey. No. 1. In traffic.
(8)	2 Bolster Wagons (4wh).	Built 1971 from redundant Morse materials for carrying rails. Dismantled 1995.
(9)	1 Open Wagon (4wh).	Supplied by R.H. Morse 1933? Scrapped.

4-Wheel Rolling Stock (9½" gauge)

Supplied by R.H. Morse. 1937; partly ex Burgoyne's railways. All sold pre-1973 being too small and delicate for DLR.

4? Open Wagons lettered DLR or SL.
1 Goods Brake Van with sanding gear lettered DLR.
1 Midland Railway Covered Van with sliding doors.
1 Cattle Van.

The Downs Light Railway Trust

THE DOWNS SCHOOL, COLWALL, MALVERN.

This is to Certify that

...... *Robert Spooner* ......

was accorded grade

..... *Two* .....

in Railway & Engineering Workshop Practice on

...... *28th July 1995* ......

on behalf of the Trustees

After a minimum of a year on the Hobby, members leaving the School qualify for this Certificate.

'It's a bit bigger than our smokebox!'. A visit to the Dowty Railway site at Ashchurch is typical of the syllabus.

J.I.C. Boyd

Index

Following the successful working parties from the Talyllyn Railway, members James Boyd and Geoffrey Naylor spent a weekend testing 'GEORGE'. The train consists of the two Parver-built flat wagons and the decorative but useless Morse-built goods brake van. 1956.

Dorothy L.E. Boyd

Aedificandum Est